Magirus
The Story of a Second-Class Citizen

Magirus

The Story of a Second-Class Citizen

CLIVE HAY

Copyright © 2016 Clive Hay

Typeset by BookPOD Pty Ltd

ISBN: 978-0-646-96367-9   eISBN: 978-1-925457-39-1

A Catalogue-in-Publication is available from the National Library of Australia.

Foreword

A few months into my national service at 1 Maintenance Unit in Kimberley I was walking past the unit hall. The sound of piano music drifted out the door - unusual in this environment, and it required investigation. I peered around the door and saw someone seated at the piano, back towards me. Something about him seemed familiar. When I approached I recognized him as Clive Hay, the author of this book. I knew Clive from our school days in Potchefstroom, where he spent two years, during which time he played in a very popular band called Jake. We greeted each other, and I was very happy to see a familiar face. We became firm friends during the next 18 months in the army. Clive's lust for life and love of music made the hardship of army life more bearable and created opportunities not normally available in those circumstances. We remain friends to this day. It was a time of contrasts, between the alien disciplinarian army environment and the alter ego of playing in a band, entertaining army and civilian alike. Through it all there was fun, adventure and exposure to new people and cultures.

I was intrigued when Clive told me he planned to write a book about his experiences in the army, and immediately tried to dredge up memories of that time in case there were any incriminating or at least embarrassing anecdotes that I may have been a part of. Sadly my memory failed me. Clive, however, has remembered those times vividly and tells the story in this engaging and entertaining book.

Alan Duke Rolstone

Preface

This is not a political book. It is, rather, a commentary on the South African Defence Force from the times of compulsory national service, as well as being a story that is close to my heart. I have tried to convey the mood and attitude of a period in my home country's history where we just had to get on with an inconvenient compromise that we all had to make in our lives.

It started about 6 years back when a blog written by fellow National Serviceman David Stevenson came to my attention. David was the guitarist for "Supertroop", the band that succeeded our band "Magirus". While it was a great blog, written with a lot of passion, I felt it completely ignored the roots and important events leading up to how Supertroop came to be allowed to function as a working band in the SANDF.

People very seldom remember pioneers. They remember the people that come AFTER the pioneering work is done - those who benefit from the groundwork laid down by the originators of so many stories. While I have great respect for Supertroop's achievements after the demise of Magirus, I felt that the foundation Magirus provided needed to be set out and understood. A lot of National Servicemen benefitted from the introduction of the army's program of Leisure Time Utilisation, and it was serendipitous that the characters in this book were there at the start of it all.

So here is our story as I remember it. It is not an exercise in one-upmanship, and I hope it doesn't come across that way. We were all extremely blessed to be doing what we loved with the time we were given.

My hope is that, when those who have done any national service read this little story, they will relate strongly to the struggles and triumphs. For everyone else, I hope you just enjoy it as an entertaining, enjoyable, romantic and informative story.

The people you will read about are real characters, in every sense of the word, and time has not diminished the love and camaraderie I feel for those I was closest to.

This young man, like so many at the time, had to negotiate his way through the minefield of young adulthood, authority and romantic intrigue – all the while stepping clumsily on the mines, but somehow surviving the blasts!

Acknowledgements

To the ladies that featured so vividly in my life at the time, each of you gave me your own distinct brand of love when I sorely needed it. Thank you. You touched my life in ways that I'll never forget.

To the families that took us in and made us feel so at home. Thank you. You provided stark relief to the sometimes unbelievable absurdity that prevailed at camp.

To my Magirus band of brothers. Thank you. There is no better thing in life than sharing musical growth and experiences, or the lifelong amity that emerged from our time together.

To my mother, Patricia Curtis, who allowed me the freedom to spread my wings without letting me fly too far out of sight. Thank you and I love you with all my heart!

Also, a big Thank You to Jennifer Stewart, not only for your copy editing skills, but also for your invaluable feedback and encouragement which helped me to dig a little deeper and come up with a few more gems for this tale.

Finally, to my wife Renata, whose love, patience and tolerance have allowed me to relive this tale when most other spouses would feel threatened and sidelined by such recollections, and my boys, Cameron, Alexander and Julian, without whom life would be diminished to a self-indulgent, fairly pointless exercise. Always know that you are the biggest part of my overall story and that you are the loves of my life!

Tribute

In memory of James Thomas, our fellow Magirus member, who died at the hands of terrorists in the Westgate shopping mall attack in Nairobi, Kenya in September 2013. He was on a mission to help others lift themselves out of poverty through education. RIP my friend.

Contents

———◆◆———

MAGIRUS

The Story of a Second-Class Citizen

———————◆◆———————

"Magirus!! The backbone of the army! That's what we're going to call this band!" Vincent and I looked at each other... Everyone else just sat there with a polite, but resigned air. I didn't like it. Vincent didn't like it. Who were we to object anyway? The army was offering us a side door to a slightly better life... We were going to open it as wide as we could! Still, I had visions of Roger Dean album covers floating through my head, and the meeting had started off with me offering some ethereal and unbelievable options, much to the amusement and denigration of the captain and those who wanted to be seen to be much more in tune with his mindset. Charles Stevens. Captain by rank, Asshole by nature. But he was all we had. And he did recognise talent. He'd put this bunch of musos together as a result of the army's new Leisure Time Utilisation program. You see, the Minister of Defence had, in his wisdom, changed the length of National Service from one year to two years in order to save South Africa from the huge Communist onslaught that was threatening the very borders of the Beloved Country. As a result, the army had to find things for us to do with the extra time they'd forced upon us. Leisure Time Utilisation was the answer, and the captain was in charge. I do think he loved Vincent. Even bought him a Fender Rhodes a bit later on, but that's all part of what I'm about to tell you...

A HINT OF THINGS TO COME

I came to the army in July of 1977—six months after completing high school—along with the rest of all the eligible white boys in the country, to do our bit. I was posted to Kimberley's 1 Maintenance Unit in the Northern Cape, five and a half hours from where I lived in Johannesburg. Like all the kids before and after me who had, at the beginning, stood on that Johannesburg train platform, waiting for their literal and metaphorical journey into the next part of their lives, I experienced a kind of nervous excitement, and the first glimpse of serious authority, in the form of what turned out to be someone I was desperately hoping I would see very little of during our basic training—Lieutenant Venter. He was a tall, sandy-haired man with a slightly bulbous nose, small unblinking eyes and a self satisfied, thin-lipped grin, exuding an air of subdued menace that made all of us quite unsettled, which was interesting, because we didn't see any rank insignia on him. We later learned that his rank was 2nd lieutenant, and that all commissioned officers wore their rank on their shoulders. (All non-commissioned officers wore their rank on their sleeve). One thing we all knew was that he was going to give anyone who was unlucky enough to get anywhere near him a difficult time!

The journey to our camp was a ten hour affair, with much talk, making new friends, covering up our fears with nervous jokes, and, of course, music. I had taken my brand new twelve string guitar along with me and was singing some of my own tunes like "Catcher in the Rye" (inspired by JD Salinger's book), "Nightdream" (which my friends at home delighted in renaming "Wetdream"), as well as some covers. On the journey we discovered that our camp's name

3

was Diskobolos. I have this habit of re-writing song lyrics of popular songs if I hear something odd or interesting sounding, like our camp's moniker, and pretty soon we were all singing "Welcome to the Hotel Disko-Bolos".

The train arrived on a freezing, misty morning, and we were herded into about fifteen of the army's staple troop mover—the Bedford truck—and driven about ten kilometres to our camp on the outskirts of town. Actually, when we were ushered into our respective companies and bungalows, I think we were all a bit surprised. With the fear of God pumped into us by our friends from previous intakes, we were expecting straw mattresses, no hot water, outside ablutions, unearthly hours of training and being yelled at from beginning to end. Instead, our corporal turned out to be a quiet-spoken man, more disposed to helping us settle in than leaving us to figure things out alone. (This was deceptive, as I was later to discover.) And our bungalows took only approximately sixteen to twenty troops, AND they had en-suite ablutions! Welcome to the Hotel Diskobolos indeed!

So all was looking quite OK to start with, except for one fly in the ointment...The discovery, the next morning, that the officer in charge of our training was a tall, sandy-haired man with a slightly bulbous nose, small unblinking eyes and a self satisfied, thin-lipped grin...That's right—our company, Maintenance 1:1, would have the dubious pleasure of being trained by none other than Lieutenant Venter!

There was one particularly ominous incident the night we arrived: at about 9pm that night, as we were unpacking and chatting amiably to each other, three corporals walked into our bungalow. We had had various instructors and ranks walking in and out as the night progressed, giving us various information and instructions, and no one felt the least disturbed or intimidated. This was different. To start with, these guys all wore sunglasses—at 9pm! They had a rather threatening-looking insignia on their arms, and as they walked in, everyone was stunned into silence. They slowly perambulated around the room, arms behind their backs, with vague grins on their faces, looking each of us in the eye as they slowly passed, like wraiths from "Lord of the Rings". Whatever they were, we knew that they were not to be dallied with. We later discovered they were PTI's—Physical Training Instructors—and whatever hell they had been though to earn their stripes, we knew we didn't want a part of it...

Basic Training was, surprisingly, a pretty routine affair: barracks and uniform inspections, learning the art of drilling, the regular 2.4 kilometre run in under twelve minutes with steel helmet, webbing and rifle (otherwise known as your kit), the onerous parades, pole PT (in which you and three others had to carry a 150 to 200 kilogram wooden telephone pole, along with your kit, for whatever distance the instructors deemed), the lectures on army rank and disciplines, the obstacle courses, the shooting range, the shouting and pouting from the NCO's, and the awful punishment at the gymnasium, hosted by—you guessed it—the dreaded PTI's! In fact, in relation to the PTI's and the punishment mentioned above, our first encounter with them in particular lives on in my memory from our basics in a way that I feel bears describing. Firstly, as a reason for the reader not to think that our entire training was easy, pedestrian and routine. And secondly, as a detailed description and precursor to an incident that occurred later in this little tale, when the newly formed Magirus had pushed the boundaries a little too far...

We had always passed the gymnasium while drilling. It was the domicile of the PTI's—where they lived, laughed, and tortured. I likened it to driving past a prison, or a boarding school. Places that you knew existed, but that you had little or no interest in getting to know on any kind of level. Places so punishing that your imagination could scarcely play out the realities of the hardships awaiting those unfortunate enough to venture inside. Yes, the gymnasium was always there, but we were only vaguely aware of its horrors, and never thought in our wildest dreams that we would go through those doors and enter into unimaginable pain...

In my mind, we were doing fine. Our morning inspections and parade drills might not have been perfect. I thought that they were acceptable. But this day was a Friday. Nothing good ever happened on a Friday in the army during basics, and when we had finished parade, a visibly irritated Lieutenant Venter seemed to have had enough. I've got to say that I always suspected that the army would work hard to make up excuses to subject us to hardships—just for the hell of it!! I don't know. Were we really that bad at everything we did? According to our lieutenant, yes we were, and we were going to be punished, although we didn't know it yet...

As we wheeled off the parade ground and marched toward our barracks, we were suddenly halted in front of the gymnasium. A conversation ensued between Venter and a PTI I hadn't seen before, and I felt the walls of doom slowly being built, brick by brick, around our little squad...I thought they were just having a conversation and a laugh at our expense. It was at our expense, but not just emotionally. The lieutenant suddenly broke off his conversation with the PTI and very angrily and loudly tree'd us on. Before we knew it we were marching through the doors of the gymnasium and being lined up in front of a rack attached to the far wall. The rack stretched from one end of the rectangular-shaped building to the other. The unfamiliar PTI rounded in front of us and, in a somewhat objective and formal manner, proceeded to inform us of the crimes of which we were accused. He sounded reasonable enough. He wasn't shouting... But out of the corner of my eye I saw a very malicious smile start curving at the corners of Lt. Venter's mouth, coupled with a rapacious glint in his eyes..."Muur toe!" (To the wall!!), came the order from the PTI, whom we now realized was in charge of this God-awful place. I snuck a look over my shoulder to see two of the PTI's from the first night in our bungalow, circling behind us, arms at the ready, looking as menacing as when we first encountered them, waiting to catch the slightest indiscretion that we might commit.

Our PTI barked out another order: "Gryp die rack en sit op julle hurke!! (Grab the rack and sit on your haunches.) Doen vir my nou tien star jumps—op my bevel" (Do ten star jumps—on my order.)

What?? Was that all?? Eeeaassyyy!!!

He counted: "Werksaam—one!" (Work together—one!)

Each member of our squad lifted himself from the haunched position while grabbing the rack, propelled himself upwards and landed back down in the haunched position. The clatter of uneven landings echoed around the room. One done!!

Again he counted, "Werksaam—one!"

We looked at each other... Surely this guy can't count??!! We launched ourselves again. Again, the thumping of uneven landings...

Again the count "One!"

I didn't cry on the train platform leaving my home for two years. I didn't cry when we did pole PT for the first time, or ran the 2.4 kilometres for the first time. Or when I worked so hard on my inspection that I got to bed at two in the morning and had to wake up at five AM for roll call. Or when I got kicked and yelled at for not saluting properly.

I cried that day! Most of us did! The number ten of our star jumps never materialized, but if we did one star jump, we did one hundred or more, broken with bouts of running around the 'Kampie' outside and back into the gymnasium to our positions on our haunches. Our legs burned—nay, were aflame—with agony!! Most of us couldn't hold ourselves up, and hung off the rack, weeping and sobbing. The complaint from our torturer was quite reasonable—we weren't working together. And until we started working together, we wouldn't get past the first star jump. Needless to say, as the torture progressed, so did our lack of co-ordination, so there was no chance of us attaining the desired perfection. After what seemed like six hours, but was, in reality, probably only an hour to an hour and a half, we staggered back outside, ragged and broken. We were marched back to our bungalows and dismissed.

Nobody spoke that weekend. Most of us lay in bed, quietly nursing our legs and, quite frankly, wondering if we would ever walk properly again. Soberly, we realized that any notion that the powers that be might be reasonable or flexible in any way, was put out of our minds once and for all...

GATHERING GLOOM

Things did get better. We got fitter and more used to the regimen of army life, and things started taking a positive direction in a small way, but one that made me think there was a glimmer of hope.

About five or six weeks into our time at the camp an announcement was made that all people who could play a musical instrument were to assemble in the Great Hall. I got there about fifteen minutes late and found myself in the middle of a pissing contest!! I met people there that I'm still friends with to this day. The first, and most noticeable one was John Ferrier. A Rock/Rock 'n Roll guitarist of note was he, and extremely determined to show off at every available opportunity—to the point of pushing into other people's playing time to try and outplay them. Needless to say, he got up my nose immediately. The second was Pete Auths, who I shall introduce you to a little later. The third was quite possibly the best guitarist I had met to date. His name was Francis Montocchio. While I could play a reasonable rendition of "Mood for a Day" and " Clap", both by Steve Howe of the band Yes, Francis could play these pieces almost perfectly—no mean feat in a world of Prog Rock. Francis, however, got posted out before we could experiment musically together, a feat we managed to achieve years later. I'm still not sure what this particular gathering was supposed to bring about, as nothing came of it. And, like Francis, the fates had other things in store for all of us. What I didn't know about that fateful day (one of a few), was that I was to be musically linked some ten months later to the one person I had no intention of being linked to—John Ferrier!

But the army was all about trying to break your spirit and co-ordinating you into one team. One of the methods used in breaking us down was simple rumour. Rumour of when and who were getting weekend passes, what happened to the guys who couldn't handle Basics, why someone got posted to camps closer to home etc. Depending on your personality type, a rumour could make or break you...

There were unspoken rules about dealing with rumours. Rumours of the Army heard OUTSIDE the Army were taken seriously... Rumours heard INSIDE the Army were to be totally ignored until you heard something from the Brass themselves. News of the possibility of extended military service came to us via the National Broadcaster in February 1977 in the form of a rumour five months before we were mustered for our national duty. The rumour proved true three months into our service. During one lunch break we all gathered around the radio to listen to the news (television was one year old in South Africa in 1977, and not broadcast during the day), as we'd heard that an announcement was going to be made regarding our new national service commitments. The newsman delivered our new jail sentence as cheerfully and calmly as if he'd announced an engagement. No one said anything. On the way back to our afternoon drill, one young Afrikaans boy broke down crying, saying to us through his tears that he loved his country, and this is how badly they treated him! Later that day I remember standing in a field adjacent to the Parade Ground, where the trains ran past, and watching a passenger train heading in the direction of Johannesburg, thinking to myself "It'll be twenty-one months before I'm on that for the last time". I couldn't remember a time before that when I'd felt such hopelessness. Worse was to come.

For every National Serviceman who came from Joburg, Pretoria was our Shangri La, our Nirvana, our Psalm 23. Oh man, the rumours abounded! Weekend passes every week, guys sleeping at home EVERY DAY and going back to camp in the mornings, four day weeks etc. etc. My dream was to get to the Entertainment Corps in Pretoria. Can you imagine it? Playing music the whole time, getting off at 1pm on Friday, spending the whole weekend at home...!

Well, I made it! almost...

One Thursday, about three weeks after the longer service announcement, and two months of rumours, we were lined up on the parade ground and divided into groups. When postings to Pretoria were called, my good friend and comrade Peter Hall and I jostled strongly together to make sure we were in the same group, and with great relief and happiness we found ourselves in the same line, heading for Shangri-La. Our group was going to Pretoria! Yeehah! I hardly slept that night from the excitement. My happiness was short lived, however...

The very next morning we were lined up on the parade ground, still excited about the previous evening's announcement, laughing and joking as the officers and NCO's came forward and silenced us. To my utter gut-wrenching dismay we were told to forget the previous day's groupings as they had to do the whole process again... Again the jostling for positions to Pretoria started, but somehow Pete and I got separated. This time Pete had made it into the Pretoria line, and I was one of three people staying in Kimberley. I stood with the other two guys in a daze and hardly listening while one of the corporals explained our future to us. I thought that I'd wake up and find I'd had a nightmare, but this was all too real. Some twenty more months of being far from home, NOT going to Pretoria, only to be allowed a weekend pass once every five to six weeks, bitterly cold winters, excruciatingly hot summers, the crass army culture, the crap food, having to kowtow to some guy with barely a primary school education just because he had a couple of stripes on his arm or a couple of stars on his shoulders. I was gutted! To make matters worse, the three of us were almost immediately posted to the petrol depot down the road to do my least favourite thing in the army—stand beat!

Standing guard, or beat as we called it, was always a Hobson's Choice. With Guard Duty came two time slots for each guard—6pm to 8pm coupled with 12am to 2am; 8pm to 10pm coupled with 2am to 4am (this one was probably the worst); and 10pm to 12am coupled with 4am to 6am. All these time slots sucked, were lonely and a bit scary, and deprived you of sleep. I remember watching the same Bedford trucks that had delivered us to our camp, leave with my friends who were on their way to Pretoria and a better situation, only sixty kilometres from home and a future doing their service I could only dream about...

When we arrived at the Depot my heart sank further. The place had three bungalows and four enormous fuel silos, and no grass— only red sand. It was devoid of any trees, and some of the guys who we were to share our duties with had clearly lost the plot. For the first time in my life I could see nothing in front of me but misery.

THE DEPOT SONG

I've written many stupid songs in my life, and "The Depot Song" was one of them. Meant to encapsulate my feelings of alienation with a bunch of misfits, it served to provide some musical comfort for my fellow Depotians, who really related to it on an immediate level. This was THEIR song! This was their "Up Yours" to the military—or at least it would have been if I had finished it... I think most of the guys there had an expectation of me completing it, which I never did. The song was in the form of a twelve bar blues, of which I had no experience in writing. Lyrically, I got as far as "This is the Depot song, this is the Depot song" and then something about everyone singing along... They all did (sing along) anyway. I suppose there have been worse pieces for people to sing to. I'll never forget being surrounded by faces in brown uniforms, me strumming away in E major, heads nodding as the words were repeated over and over, faces staring expectantly at me for the next line of the song, which never appeared...

The Depot marked a distinct downturn in my life, not only musically, but socially too. I managed to alienate myself from my fellow inmates as the weeks wore on, and I think we were all going quite mental as a result of the boredom and repetition of our mundane duties. The guys I bunked with ranged from self-styled pseudo philosophers (if you could call their views on everything "philosophy"), regular people and gentle, well meaning types; to quite sociopathic individuals whom I secretly despised, although I wisely kept my opinions about them to myself. I have to emphasize here that I didn't think myself better than any of them—au contraire I've always been fascinated by different personality types, and always

13

impressed and surprised by people when I got to know them. Being impressed by some types of people, however, didn't necessarily place them in my "awe" category, although a lot of them obviously thought it did. No, I'm merely a student of human nature with my own weaknesses and failings. I think the difference between them and me in those days was that I had no desire to make myself out to be anything but what I knew I was. But it was my secret distaste for some of the more unsavoury aspects of people's natures and habits that would lead me to situations that I tried to avoid, and one habit in particular that would draw me unwittingly into conflict and disparagement with both the Depotians and the Military Police... The whole "dope" thing.

Our daily routine was, quite frankly, mind numbing. To be honest, I can't even remember whether we ate at the Depot or at the main camp—that's how much of an impression the food and our routine left on me. We were un-chaperoned during the day, and I do remember a lot of lying around in our bungalows, being coerced into ganging up on people others didn't like, and sleeping through a lot of our sentry duties (the second shift ones in particular). When the Permanent Force officers did decide to check on us, we were always being punished for our indiscretions and failed inspections with forced marches, extra guard duties, longer PT routines and extra drills.

Where the dope trouble started was with the impression our military masters had of us being pot heads. The reason they had that impression was that a lot of the guys, (including myself albeit very rarely, and preferably as a social thing and out of uniform), DID partake, and, to make matters worse, they were pretty keen for people—anyone, really—to KNOW that they were "different", and as a result, "cool". There was nothing cool about being in the army, so this was their way of saying to people "Hey man, we might be in uniform, but (nudge nudge), just look at our poses, our red eyes, and in particular, listen to the way we talk—we're cool!" I have to state here that I enjoyed Cheech and Chong and found pop comedy of the day really funny, but I never subscribed to their lifestyle. I have never had to try and be cool, mainly because I never WAS cool to begin with, and never had any ambition to be one of the guys. I have always been for the most part a non-conformist, which meant that I didn't conform to both conformists AND non-conformists. The latter conformed to whatever they thought a non-conformist would do anyway! Living in South Africa in the 70's meant you were basically one of two types of people: the first was your regular "good ol' boy" who towed the party line, loved his school, sports and country, was clean living and conformed to the norms of the crowd, and was heading for a bright future armed with a university degree. The second was the cool fringe types that I described above. These days people would probably divide them into Jocks and Nerds, but in South Africa at that time, people who were jocks were just as nerdy and studious as the more homely individuals. The dope heads were sort of average intelligence, but extremely stereotyped, without realising it. Myself and a few others fitted somewhere between the two and were either liked or despised by both.

There were two people at the Depot who I was going to spend the rest of my service with, although I didn't know it at the time. One of these was a wonderful but very melancholic human being by the name of Pete Auths. Pete was a piano player, who was very popular with the easy to impress set because he was the Arpeggio King. Doing things in measured themes, musically-speaking, was not in his repertoire when I first met him. Over-embellishment got the required reaction from the punters. He was good, but I felt that his over-compensating playing was totally unnecessary and ruined what could have been great musical interpretation. The other was Kevin Jarman. Kevin was someone I took a liking to almost immediately. He was a very talented singer and guitarist who sounded just like Joe Walsh from the Eagles; we would have long conversations about everything and nothing, loved jamming together and just were generally pretty comfortable around each other. There was, however, a flaw in his character (and mine) which led to an incident that changed our friendship, as I shall explain...

As the weeks turned into months, things got steadily worse. Christmas was coming up and I was hoping to get a weekend pass so I could get back to Joburg and go out with my friends. There we would often frequent a disco called "The Boat", which was a building shaped like a boat and had various "decks" and a main "cabin". It was a great place to party and release our testosterone. Sadly, Christmas for me was spent at the Depot. A sorrier Christmas I never had. I did manage to get out on the New Year's weekend and decided to invite Kevin home with me. The weekend started great, with us hitch-hiking home, going out on Saturday to my local shopping mall and me introducing him to my friends at home. We went to The Boat that Saturday night and a great time was had by all. I was going to be the toast of the Depot when we got back to Kimberley, with Kev singing my praises as "the 'oke' to be with", and "if you want a REAL joll (good time), go to Clive's place"... Or so I thought... Everyone got a bit drunk and was acting stupidly. No problem there. The problem was that when Kevin got drunk he would get aggressive, and the person he picked on was a good friend of mine Mally, who happened to be our ride home. Kevin got kicked out of the car, Mally screamed off at 120 kilometres per hour with me in the front seat leaving Kevin alone and stranded about twenty-five kilometres from my place in totally unfamiliar territory at 12am. I half heartedly asked Mally to go and pick him up (to which he said an emphatic "No!"), but the truth was, I was really pissed off at Kevin. He'd ruined a perfectly good evening, and by extension, weekend, and threatened my ride home. I didn't see why I should be stranded with him so late at night and so far from the comfort of my bed just because at the last minute he decided that the best way to end the evening was violently.

After a good night's sleep, I spent the whole morning looking for Kevin who had, in the meantime, eventually made his way to my house. Where he'd spent that night is a mystery to me until today. To say he was annoyed with me is an understatement of note. He didn't talk to me for two days and when we got back to the Depot he succeeded in painting himself as the victim in all this, and me the heartless asshole. Truth is, we probably both acted like assholes, but as we all know, hindsight is a regretful teacher. We never had the same open talks after that, and I don't think we trusted each other as much. A real pity, as we had a great friendship. But our history together was far from over...

BACK TO BASICS

In the meantime, back once again at the Depot, things had gotten so bad with regard to our attitudes and actions in doing our guard duties that the company's officers had reached a decision to return us to the main camp. This was in February of 1978. The great petrol guarding enterprise had failed dismally, and we sensed that the Brass were incensed! Well, they didn't mince their words as to what they thought of us. I must mention here that the South African Defence Force relied on Permanent Force members (hereafter referred to by the abbreviation "PF's") to run their camps and oversee the national servicemen and their duties. These PF's were, in general, not particularly ambitious individuals who regarded national servicemen as their personal servants, there to do whatever they deemed was too difficult or too much trouble for themselves. Because the whole country was run on a "buddy" system, a great deal of inept, bigoted and incompetent people came to be in charge of the multitudes. This applied not only to the armed forces, but to the country's very leadership. Our direct contact, however, was within the confines of One Maintenance Unit. This situation was, in fact, a blessing in disguise which we were only too happy to use to our own advantage whenever, wherever and however we could. Don't get me wrong—it wasn't a cakewalk! Most military organisations have strict disciplinary codes which are adhered to rigidly, and this was no exception. Because of our two years' service, we just had the extra time on our hands to learn how to use the system to our advantage.

Incredibly, in many ways our start at the main camp was more dismal than being at the Depot. Here we were surrounded by authority, whereas at the Depot we were our own bosses to a large extent. We were also re-introduced to the dirge and ridiculousness of Friday Parade—what a crock. (Little did I know that within a few weeks, I would be delivered from Parades forever). Parade was invented by people with a lot of time on their hands who loved to shout and scream a lot, walk up behind helpless troops and whisper obscenities in their ears and generally waste our time by lining us up, inspecting us and marching us round in squares. I hated Parade almost as much as second shift on guard duty. We were also introduced to our daily work detail. Some guys got great jobs which were easy to do and enjoy, like the armoury, or clerical jobs. Most of us Depotians were assigned to the Transport Park.

It was at this point that things got decidedly worse for me, and I reached the lowest ebb in my time at Kimberley.

KAFFERTJIE DE MEYER, GREG THE SELF-RIGHTEOUS AND INSPECTOR CLUES-OU

B eing genetically made up as a muso has left me with distinct disadvantages in the world of Real Men. To start with, I'm not much of a sportsman and after primary school I decided that the country could do without one more Rugby or Cricket player and that there were other ways to attract women besides these pastimes. Secondly, and this is pivotal to this chapter of my story, I'm not mechanically minded and have limited interest in motor vehicles in general apart from as a means of transportation. I can perform routine maintenance, like changing flat tyres, changing headlight bulbs and a few really small things that require me looking under the bonnet, like checking the oil and water. Do not ask me to perform grease and oil changes or anything that requires, in my mind, a degree in mechanical engineering. I simply don't expend my thoughts or energies in those areas.

So I experienced great trepidation when I was assigned to maintaining the camp's Bedford trucks in the Transport Park, under the psychotic eye of one Sergeant Major 2nd class de Meyer. This was a guy who had short man's syndrome to the worst possible degree. Probably the most short-tempered, intolerant, aggressive and small minded individual I have ever met. I do have to say that he was universally disliked by troops and brass alike because of these personality traits. He was also quite dark skinned and this, as a result, along with his lack of height, must have been the source of tremendous bullying in his youth by a people and culture that could find no redeeming qualities in this kind of physical makeup. It must have led to the worst nicknames too, and one that he certainly brought with him from somewhere along his journey. In our camp, he was simply known as Kaffertjie! I could almost feel sorry for him when I think of how this name, which is a derogatory term for blacks in South Africa, would have affected his life if it, or similar monikers, had been used while growing up in such a polarised society.

He had, however, risen to the aforementioned rank, which had, in turn, given him a disproportionate amount of power over us lesser individuals. This he abused with reckless abandon, and when you have two people with such large personality differences in such a situation, you can only have one outcome. To say I liked the Transport Park is akin to saying Salieri liked Mozart (see the movie "Amadeus"). I would've been happier doing PT with the PTI's twice a day! (Well, on second thoughts maybe I'm exaggerating).

One day, while doing the most mind-numbing task of filling truck batteries with water, I noticed a lieutenant with blonde hair, moustache and glasses wandering into our section of the Transport Park. He had a brief chat with Kaffertjie and then proceeded to call one of our Depot guys aside to the office for a quiet chat. He then came out after dismissing the aforementioned person and called another person in. And so it went until it was my turn. By this time I was aware of the nature of this procedure, and was extremely nervous. I was about to be questioned about the Depot's dope habits, by a self-appointed army detective who was relishing his role as an Afrikaans Mike Hammer, but was more like Inspector Clouseau in his actions and questioning style. His name was Lieutenant Francois Malan. I was made to feel relatively at ease in his presence, and the questions were fairly innocuous:

"Do you know of anyone who might have brought dagga into the Camp?" "No".

"Have you ever smoked it yourself?" "Yes, but not in the army".

"Do you know if anybody else in your crowd smokes it outside the army?" "I'm sure a lot of the guys might have done it at some stage, but I don't know who."

In my innocence, I didn't realise that answering these last two questions in the affirmative was going to make me extremely unpopular with the Depotian Dope Heads!

The next couple of weeks are a bit of a blur to me, but what I do remember is that I was suddenly seen by most of my colleagues as some kind of snitch/informer to the detective. My protests to the contrary were largely ignored, and my character and loyalty called into question by a self-appointed arbiter of Depot justice, a guy by the name of Greg Simpson. This was a sad turn of events because I quite liked Greg. He was an affable surfer boy from the Eastern Cape who thought he was pretty cool, and who liked to toe the Depot line of coolness as depicted in my earlier chapter. He did strike me as the kind of guy, however, who would make allegiances according to what or who was cool and in flavour as opposed to what he REALLY thought of a situation or person, and he LOVED an audience! And so, with these new dramas, he chose to become my enemy. It started one day in the Transport Park with a self-righteous tirade about what an asshole I was for "betraying" the guys, and continued at various intervals throughout the next few weeks where it escalated into physical threats—always with an audience, of course. I felt very alone and despised. It seemed that everyone felt the same about me, and a lot of the feeling had to do with the Kevin episode at The Boat, which had leaked out and which made me out to be the bad guy. With hindsight, people are people, and everyone needs a scapegoat in such a situation—I just didn't like the fact that it was me!

The final escalation to the drama came after a few weeks of Lt. Malan's ongoing investigations. It was all bullshit of course—he LOVED being a detective and really thought he was pretty clever, relishing his role as an Afrikaans Inspector Morse, having read one too many Sherlock Holmes stories. One day, one of the guys and myself were asked to report to his office at lunchtime. I was both apprehensive and annoyed. We had little time to relax as it was, without more inane questioning...and that during our lunch break!

We knocked on the door and were invited inside, and here's where it got interesting. I have to point out here that my apprehension was more about having to deal with a military tribunal than dealing with him—I had no fear of him as a person. The questions started: names, dates, places… By this time I was used to his line of questioning, and at the same time I was trying to impress on the Depotians that I was to be trusted in these situations. What happened next surprised (and somewhat amused) me!

The questions stalled, so the lieutenant got up and walked over to the windows and closed the curtains. He then proceeded to the door and locked it. I was sitting in a chair facing his desk, with my compatriot seated near me. Very suddenly, my chair was pulled violently around and a paper knife shoved in front of my face. The look on my friend's face was priceless. A verbal tirade ensued, peppered with threats. What was said actually left me feeling strangely defiant, and not intimidated. This was mainly because nobody really took this guy too seriously. I responded with the air of an innocent martyr, who was guilty of no crime except being in the wrong place and in the wrong company. I was told that unless I produced evidence, that I was in a lot of trouble!!

The problem for my tormentor was that we both knew, within one minute of him taking this line, that he had lost the moral high ground. And a few minutes later, after a spirited defence from me, I was facing a frustrated but ultimately defeated man. We were shown the door.

The news of my gritty buttress against the Keystone Cop was greeted with muted indifference by the Depotians. What did I expect, a medal? According to them I wasn't cool, anyway, man! But in some ways it neutralised their skewed sense of justice—they were, after all, engaged in an illegal activity, whichever way they saw it! There's just no pleasing some people…

As a postscript to this whole sorry saga, about a month later I was stopped by Lt. Malan and was given a short but friendly lecture on the dangers of "dagga" (marijuana, for non-South Africans), and that I should choose my company more carefully. What? Was he kidding? The army chooses your company, you don't!! Anyway, I acceded in the name of good manners and moved on... And things were going to start getting better.

LEISURE TIME UTILISATION

About two weeks after the knife incident, our sorry bunch were called to the gymnasium for an announcement. While we waited there, a few boxing matches were being fought in an improvised ring, with one guy in particular displaying some great footwork and defensive skills. Eventually, Greg challenged me to a bout, which I wisely declined, as he was a fairly well proportioned individual and I was as skinny as a rake! There was the general laughing scorn, which rolled off my back—I'm not an idiot, after all. As the morning ensued, a medium sized officer with dark hair, piercing eyes, moustache and three captain's stars on his shoulders moved into the gym, during which time we all stood as he headed for the boxing ring. This man was about to play a major role in the rest of our army life... This was Captain Charles Stevens!! He mounted the podium and read the following announcement: our camp was looking to form a band, and auditions were going to be held the next day. Whoever could play an instrument was ordered to report to the gymnasium. There was a general buzz, and not a small amount of excitement. Actually, there weren't that many musos in our camp, and of the few there were, most were not remarkable. There were of course, exceptions.

Audition day rolled around without fanfare... What fanfare? We were in the army! After breakfast, we all headed off to the gym. There was an element of fun in the air, and the Depotians, as well as the rest of the camp, were sitting in groups, talking, laughing, complaining. The captain and his sidekicks all came in and the usual hush, saluting and murmuring ensued. The musicians were then told to get up and start performing. A drum set, an organ, a couple of amps and a PA system had been provided. For some reason, the person who stood out most to me that day was Pete Auths. We were at the Depot together, and here we were playing music. Pete definitely had a presence and some ability. I can't remember what we sang (I seem to remember doing an Eagles number), but it obviously impressed the captain. As soon as we had finished playing, another guy got up and headed for the keyboard. He sat down with a couple of other guys and they started playing... Very impressive performance—fair vocally, but he played proficiently and was obviously a well-versed muso. This was my introduction to Vincent. The guy on the drums was a standout. His name was Eddie Prinsloo and, as fate would have it, we would be working together for the best part of a year. Eddie and I would develop a love/hate relationship over this period, but ultimately, we remained firm friends.

When their performance was over, the captain headed down towards us and gathered us around. In a crisp, commanding tone he informed Vincent and me that there were to be two bands—I would be in charge of one, and Vincent would be in charge of the other! We were free to choose our own members. There would be ten of us initially in the whole Leisure Time Utilisation program, with a few more to follow! This was exciting news for everyone, and immediately people were lobbying for positions in the band. Almost immediately I was surrounded by some of the Depotians, who had decided that in order to make up for my sins, the best thing I could do was take on Kevin as a part of my band. This was a thorny issue. Things were not right between Kevin and me, and in the past when choosing band mates, I was not one to take on people I thought would be a liability. This was emotional blackmail. It's not that he couldn't do the job. I just wondered how well we would work together in light of the previous circumstances, and besides, he struck me as being undisciplined and a "user" to boot! A few weeks earlier he had taken some "mal pitte" seeds that had put him out of action and into orbit for three days! And to be honest, he had a much higher vocal range than me and I was a tiny bit jealous of his capabilities. But he had talent that I would have been foolish to ignore, and so Kevin became a part of my band.

The rest of my band was made up by drummer Eddie and Pete Auths on keys. While trying to work out who was going to be our bass guitarist, I was called aside by the captain and informed that he had already chosen one for us. His name was Des Hadlow, and he held the rank of corporal. We were told that, while Vincent and I were theoretically in charge of our bands, Des was ACTUALLY in charge of both bands due to the fact that he was a Permanent Force member. A Permanent Force member, we were told, would bring stability and the right sort of order to us National Servicemen! Stability and order... Little did we know...

My new found status as band leader gave me a new sense of hope for the long days ahead, and I decided that it was time for a change of job. Kaffertjie and I were butting heads on almost a daily basis, and this would climax in some kind of huge drama, of which I'd had more than my fair share over the last few months. My strategy was to approach the captain and ask him for a transfer to his unit's office— he was OC of Transport 1:1 and seriously outranked Kaffertjie. After all, I reasoned, he did like me somewhat, and I thought that striking while the iron was hot would work in my favour. I wasn't wrong—I can be quite charming and persuasive in the right situations—and things seemed to be going in the right direction. Within the week I had secured a new position as one of the captain's Company Clerks and was ordered to report to my new job in a few days—and what a cushy job it was! Needless to say, Sergeant Major 2nd class Kaffertjie De Meyer was furious. How dare anyone "steal" any of his troops from the Transport Park! He yelled some obscenities at me. I feigned innocence—"I'm not responsible for transfers within the camp. The captain obviously needed a company clerk and I was the one chosen." He complained to one of the majors at HQ, who didn't want to know anything about this and washed his hands of the situation. Obviously, this transfer had been effected over the sergeant major's head, and he was NOT pleased. "Get out of my sight!!" This was not the last time I was going to hear these words from him...

SETTLING IN—THE
PHONEY MONTHS

———————◆◄———————

After doing manual labour in the transport park for close to two months, reporting to the captain for my duties was akin to being let out of a Siberian Gulag and being ushered into the Waldorf... Well, maybe that's an exaggeration, but you get my drift. My principle duties were roll call, reporting the company strength to the camp HQ, taking phone calls and general paperwork. This was peppered with rehearsal sessions with the two bands, which usually took place after lunch for about two hours. By this time, most of the band members had been settled into their new duties, but in my band the captain insisted that two more additions had to be made. The first time I had any inkling of this was one day, as I was thumping out some tunes on the piano in the hall, a few guys from the new January 1978 intake came in to have a listen. "Poor sods!" I thought. " They'll still have six months stuck in this place after I leave!" Then suddenly, one of them leaned forward and called out quietly, "Clive!" I turned and saw a person who has turned out to be one of my closest friends from that time onwards, Alan Rolstone. Alan and I were at school together in a small town in the Western Transvaal, but he was in a higher year than me, and I was boarding at the school while he was a day student living in that town. Consequently, we knew each other but seldom talked, mainly due to the seniority situation at the school. He had spent two years studying at Pietermaritzburg University before dropping out and finally being called up. Alan was a Cornet player, and a very competent one at that; he could do something I couldn't—read a chart! He was good friends with another new guy, a friendly and jovial, ruddy-faced Capetonian by the name of

James Thomas, who played the trumpet. These two were soon-to-be members of my band... It was the first time I had ever been in charge of a band with a brass section.

Vincent's eventual band line-up consisted of five guys: Ian van der Linde on guitar, Nick Vlok on drums, Malcolm Aberdeen on Bass and Hugh van Tonder on organ. Two of the earlier members, Mungo Park (guitar) and Gary Jarvis (bass guitar), got transferred out shortly after our premier performance for the PF's - but more of that first performance in the following chapter! A few notes on the guys in Vincent's band: Ian was a very likeable and sunny type with an infectious sense of humour. He was very bright and played a pretty fair guitar. The only thing that bothered the rest of us slightly was that he had a non-sexual crush on Vincent. I hasten to add that it didn't bother Vincent who lapped up every bit of attention lavished on him by anyone. Every lunch break in the band bungalow after we'd eaten, we'd lie on our beds, drowsily waiting to return to our duties. Vince would regale us all with stories of his female conquests, how big his gelong was, how many pro gigs he'd already done, and how much music gear he possessed. Ian would be seated front row centre, enthralled! Alan and I would get bored with the boasting and pass out. I would occasionally peek at the congregation of the faithful, and Vincent would always be looking in our direction to see if we were listening.

Nick was quiet and easy going, and approached his drums in the same manner. Malcolm, oh Malcolm. Very friendly. In fact the first time I met him, we got on like a house on fire and had a very interesting two hour-long conversation about life, the universe, and all sorts of transcendental subjects. The problem was that, in subsequent meetings, the nature of the conversation never changed—neither did the time that was taken to talk about it!

Hugh was a guy who I was going to spend a lot of time with— we both worked together as company clerks for the captain. He was one serious person, with occasional lapses into humour. He was one of those people around whom one was careful with one's words and facial expressions, lest they think you didn't like them—

quite sensitive and always eager to prove himself the man. I did like him, and when he let fly with the humour he had some clangers! But sometimes being around him was like sailing the seas with a hold full of nitroglycerine during a cyclone! As far as his playing ability was concerned, he was an adequate organ player—I would even venture to say that he learnt his trade by the motto "If you can point a finger, you can play a Lowrey" (which, by the way, was an old advert for that make of organ.)

Poetry abounded in those early months, partly from boredom, partly from a sense of youthful perversion. Three poems spring to mind, two of them courtesy of Hugh, written in Afrikaans:

SOMER (Summer)
Dit is Somer
En dit is vokken warm
WINTER (Winter)
Dit is Winter
En dit is vokken koud
The third, written by my best mate, Alan:
(No title)
Outside the snow lay thick
He had nothing to live for
Disrobed, he opened the door
The cold wind froze his prick
And the wind cries, "More!"

The humour and deadpan manner they were delivered in has never ceased to make me laugh aloud when I've imparted these poems to friends, and were a symbol of the start of a long, joyful time of tight fraternity between "Die Band", as we were known with disdain and grudging respect amongst PF's and national servicemen of all ranks. We looked out for each other in every respect, and abused whatever service we were entered into by the army, to make sure our little band benefited above and beyond the permitted boundaries...

I was a novice at AWOL-ing. It took Vincent and Ian to coax me into doing it the first time. (For the uninitiated, AWOL is a military term for Absent WithOut Leave). It required a few subtleties that most guys in the army never quite got right. Rule number one was, Never AWOL In Your Uniform. If you did, the MP's (military police) would almost certainly stop you, question you and, ultimately, charge you—after which you were a marked man! If you AWOL-ed in your civvies, you would be taken for an officer or a PF and consequently left alone. The second rule was, Don't Act Like You're New At This. Most servicemen who were allowed to be out of the camp acted just like that—that they were allowed to be out of the camp! If you acted guilty, shy or awkward in any way, you were a sure-fire target for the authorities. Third rule: Make Sure You Have A Backup Plan. Ours was our band members who wouldn't take the chance to follow in our footsteps. They were loyal, punctual and had the phone numbers of all of our girlfriends... But more of that later. A quick aside regarding girls:

During one of my early AWOL jaunts, I was entering the centre of town when I saw a girl whom Alan and I knew from boarding school days. Her name was Diane Warner and I'd always had a small crush on her. She was busy crossing the road when I told our driver to hoot. He did, and got a very angry response from her. As we were moving, and I was on her opposite side by this time, I couldn't lean out the window and shout. When we returned to camp I very excitedly told Alan that I was sure I'd seen her, but he thought I'd seen a ghost. A quick look in the phone book (there weren't too many Warners in Kimberley) and a few phone calls confirmed my sighting as positive. That wasn't the last we saw of Diane.

AWOL-ing was a risky business and I did get caught a couple of times, but without much consequence. The first time was the scariest. I went with Ian and Vincent into town, and remember being almost speechless with fear every time we passed anything that looked remotely military—cars, people, M.P.'s... I made it back in one piece, however, and was hooked from that day on. It was early days still, but because I'd found my nerve with the AWOL story and its nuances, I was beginning to get really casual about the way I conducted myself around the camp, which led me to probably the closest shave I'd had with authority in my new found freedom.

I happened to be on Company Duty one Monday night, but had finished Roll Call, changed into my civvies and was about to hit the town when the Officer on Duty sent a Roof (new intake guy) to look for me. All of the band were good friends with most of the national service officers, and they generally turned a blind eye to us going out; a privilege afforded strictly to them and any PF members. There were a couple of new kids on the block, however, who didn't know of our unspoken arrangement, and who were also quite paraat (adhering strictly to the rules). The officer on duty that night was a new boy, 2nd Lieutenant Mark Freyne, and what I'd seen of him and his interaction with regular national servicemen around the camp did not fill me with confidence.

Very nervously, I made my way to the duty office, which was located right at the main gate, only to find him walking very fast in my direction:

"Are you the corporal on duty?" "Yes Lieutenant..." (I wasn't a corporal yet, but was awaiting my stripes.)

Pause...look of some confusion on his face...should he say something to me, bawl me out, what would the other looties say to him if he did? Would it be very uncool to crap out one of the band guys? (He knew who we were—the whole camp knew who we were by that time). I will never forget that pause. My life hung there in the balance...I would never be able to AWOL again, and I had some sixteen months left of service... Remember, I was in my civvies... "Could you please find Private Langeveld for me—he's got an urgent phone call up at the duty room from his mother."

Never in my army career was I so happy to obey an order. I must have found Private Langeveld in one minute flat, and as I sprinted off towards his bungalow, I knew that I was in the clear, and would remain so the rest of my army life. I went out after delivering the private to the duty office and celebrated!

By this time the band had all settled into their army day jobs. Hugh and I continued with our work for the captain as his company clerks. Our position was quite important, because we were in charge of the weekend pass books—official leave, that is—and after filling out the respective pass for a soldier and signing it, we would just require an officers' signature to make it official. This system was ritualistically abused, particularly by yours truly—like the time I signed myself out for two four-day long weekends in a row, returning after the second long weekend to my post in the face of death-stares from the captain, but amazingly, no rebuke—but became less important as we settled down to life in Kimberley with our respective girlfriends and social circles as time wore on (more later...). The other guys had settled into various other positions like Alan and Pete at the pay office, a couple of guys at the NSM registry, Dave Oldham (Des Hadlow's eventual replacement and whom I shall get to in due course), some guys at the Stores and a few in the Transport Park. The PF's and officers used to call us the Mafia, because we had guys in almost every sector of the camp that counted. One of the highest compliments we got was from a young Jewish national serviceman at our camp who lived in Kimberley. He said we would make great Jews because we had a hand in almost every part of the camp, and that's why people hated us so much... Our day jobs, however, were soon going to be augmented by the very reason music was introduced to our routine in the first place.

A FIRM CONSTITUTION AND
PLAYING FOR THE PF'S

C ountries have constitutions, maybe even large corporations. But bands? Apparently, in the army when you have a captain with delusions of grandeur, a constitution is required. Whether one actually follows the constitution or not is arguable at best, but a constitution was required, and a constitution was hammered out. What did it propose? Honestly? I seem to remember that a lot of stuff was said about how we as Soldiers of "Ons Land" (Our Country) had to conduct ourselves accordingly, blah, blah, blah, dress etc. I was feigning interest, and, being English-speaking, my opinion was not readily sought-after anyway. I remember the meeting, though, sitting listening to the drivel that was supposed to make us be amazed that such an idea could even be imparted to mere NSM's. Then came the name of the band. It was supposed to be a democratic decision, but was, as I explained at the beginning, made by the captain on his own with our implicit "approval". We were also introduced to our "band uniform". It consisted of what in effect was a track suit, with the unit's logo brandished on our left breast, with a wide collar. It was a cross between royal and navy blue with two yellow stripes running down both arms, and another two running down the outer part of each leg. We looked like we'd been dressed by our mothers.

It had been awhile since we had been put together—at least three to four weeks—and we were beginning to wonder whether or not we were going to perform for anyone at all, when the captain finally announced our first gig. We were seriously excited at the prospect of playing for ANYONE. We soon learned the perils of such thinking...

Our first gig was going to be a "Bring and Braai" for the PF's in the camp's hall. These took place twice a month on a Friday. Since it was our premier appearance, the captain had decided to organize a press night on our debut, to introduce us to Kimberley society via the local media. Great excitement ensued at this piece of news! We were told that the purpose of this was to let everyone in the vicinity know that the army was utilizing the extra time forced on its citizens in a meaningful way. The only sour note was that when the local newspaper, the Diamond Fields Advertiser, reported our evening, Vincent's band was billed as "Band number one" and my band as "Band number two". This despite the fact that my band had a brass section and two more members than Vincent's band!! I could see the captain's favouritism starting to creep in, and I was, frankly, put out! There was no difference between us musically—we both had great strengths, and both bands impressed our observers on the night. It wasn't a biggie, but it rankled us somewhat.

I have to point out here that, being young and highly idealistic, I had visions of doing all the music that I loved, and it being accepted enthusiastically by our audience. Oh, boy...

To say we weren't prepared for our audience is on a par with saying Russia wasn't prepared when the Nazis invaded. Oh, we had a repertoire, but it wasn't anything like what was expected. Fortunately we had a few guys who could play Boeremusiek (Afrikaans folk music) standards, which, unbeknownst to me, was almost all that was required by our "audience".

Our "audience"... This consisted of people we feared during the day because of their rank and status in the camp, and who we feared at night because they got blind drunk, abused their position and, as a result, us. They would invade the stage and our personal space, and sometimes even assaulted us if the current song we were playing wasn't to their liking. I think it's fair to say that these people were really the dregs of society who, because they had some authority in the army, wrongly assumed they had some standing in regular society; that is, if they could stand at all during these events. These were crass mockers, bullies and general low-lifes who pulled rank if you showed any sign of dissent. Playing in high school bands was by far preferable to this. This description might seem harsh, but I think it's fair to liken them to football hooligans.

A gig was a gig, however, and we busied ourselves with the task of playing and singing as best we could. Both bands worked together as one unit that night. I was using a Stratocaster copy—the actual brand name escapes me—and most of the other gear (drums, organ, bass guitar and some amps) was supplied by the army. There was quite a buzz as we set up. The day before, we had drawn up a (rather unrealistic as it turned out) repertoire list for the event—stuff like "Lyin' Eyes" by the Eagles, old standards like "Summertime", "Whiter Shade of Pale" and "Apache". To be fair, most of this went down OK, but as the drink flowed, so the call for Boeremusiek got more strident...and little prepared us for what was to follow in our last two sets... Much to our discomfort and dismay, it appeared that our bass player, and man responsible for us, Des Hadlow, had a drinking problem. This became apparent to us when the notes he played in these final two sets were not performed in their right spot in the song we were performing, or at best, they were played a semitone up or down from the original note intended. Des' favourite show piece was a souped-up version of "(How Much Is) That Doggie in the Window". We would start it off slowly, a la the original, and then surprise our audience by launching into a Rock 'n Roll onslaught, complete with crashing drums, crashing guitars, crashing brass and finally, a very drunk bass guitarist/singer falling off the stage and crashing out of the entire song. Even though this turned out to be a regular occurrence at these events, by some miracle on our "Big Night", The Diamond Fields Advertiser reporters had left before any damage could be done to the band's reputation.

After our debut, the next Bring and Braais's for the PF's were mediocre affairs, with us trying to accommodate the requirements of the "Elite". These guys also fancied themselves as first rate dancers, which amused me no end. A song would start, and if they liked it they would literally pull their bemused partners onto the dance floor, flinging them around with controlled passion and very serious, stony looks on their faces as if to say, "You want to see dancing? I'll show you dancing!!", and "I can see you looking at me, but I'll pretend I don't see you watching my AMAZING moves!" The arrogance was palpable, and the fact that they thought everyone took them so seriously was laughable.

Interestingly, besides the first one, I don't remember Captain Stevens being present at any of these functions. I'm pretty sure he must have been at a few of them, but he didn't make his presence felt that readily.

BECOMING A FAMILY

A nother interesting development was when the captain decided that the band needed to be housed in one bungalow—all fifteen of us—together—in one room! I think I can safely say that it was tantamount to putting a bunch of mischievous chimps in one enclosure. But boy, did we have fun! Aside from AWOL-ing almost every night, there were water fights, pillow fights, raucous arguments, uncontrolled laughter and general mayhem—and every one of us loved every minute of it! As it was my job to count and deliver the company strength to HQ when I was rostered for that duty (usually once a week on a fortnightly basis), the job sequestered me somewhat from the band bungalow to the duty room. As I mentioned earlier, part of my duty was to take evening roll call at 9pm (refer to my earlier incident with Lieutenant Frayne). Then in the morning I had to be up at 4:30am take roll call at 5am, and so lose valuable sleep time. I soon got around these little headaches by getting the most enthusiastic new boys in each bungalow to do the roll call books for me, then deliver them to the duty room, enabling me to AWOL if I wanted to, as well as sleep in the next morning. I have to point out here that when I had my little system down to a fine art, doing duty was infinitely preferable in most ways than regular army routine. The duty room was a wonderful little room, with a fan for summer, and a heater for winter. It had a single bed with a couple of extra blankets, and someone always had food lying around. The best part was that I could sleep an hour longer than everyone else once I'd received the roll call books. All I had to do was count the strength, record it on the official document and deliver it to HQ, and that I always did at 7am—one hour after everyone else in our band bungalow was supposed to have risen, and two hours after the new boys, or "Roofs" (Afrikaans for "scabs") as we called them, had risen. Furthermore, I wasn't subject to any bungalow inspection. Inspection was a big deal in the army, and a thing to be feared. Wednesday was a minor inspection day, usually carried out by a 2nd or full lieutenant. Friday was the big deal, where a captain or major would do the honours. If a bungalow or individual didn't measure up, there would be hell to pay! Many a time during my basic training, inspection did not measure up to the standard required. And consequently, harsh punishments were meted out to the whole company. One time during basics, our CO was so disgusted with us that he ordered a sixteen kilometre route march with full kit and rifle, and the added weight of an extremely heavy wooden telephone pole—four troops to a pole—which was to be carried on our shoulders while we ran! Needless to say, most people had differing levels of rhythm, stamina and strength, resulting in the pole bouncing up and down mercilessly on our shoulders, falling off, and pulling people to the ground left, right and centre! As I mentioned in Chapter 1, failing inspection was not a smart thing to do, as my band colleagues would soon find out...

In the meantime, however, life was peachy and the world was invariably our oyster. One memorable night, we tree'd each other on (called ourselves into marching order), dressed in nothing but our underwear, with brooms and shovels as rifles, and with much yelling and screaming, marched ourselves in as disorderly a way as we could around the company bungalows in mock seriousness, much to the amazement and amusement of the roofs and the duty officer. Everyone thought we were genuinely certifiable, and I know that most of the ranks had, if not a genuine liking for us, then at least a grudging respect for the way we cocked a snook at the system.

My favourite trick when I was duty bound was to rouse my band mates on my morning rounds with my version of a Genesis song, "I Know What I Like". I would yell the first line of the song through the window with amendments to the original lyrics—"It's one o'clock and time for lunch, dum de dum de dum dum" became "It's six o' clock and time to get up, dum de dum de dum dum". I would be greeted back with yells, expletives and flying boots by guys who should have risen at least fifteen minutes prior. One of our company lieutenants , and the captain's right hand man—Lieutenant Breedt— was a genuinely nice Afrikaans man, who we all took advantage of whenever we could. He did have his limits, though, and one day, after some indiscretion on my part, I was given three extra duties, then a week's worth for answering back, and finally, two weeks' extra duties for protesting. I was, at first, a little put out, but due to the routine I'd developed, it turned into a pleasure camp for yours truly, and, sinisterly, my saving grace...

One Wednesday morning, as I was doing my duty rounds, I passed by our barracks and stuck my head in to torment everyone with my usual greeting. I was greeted in turn with the usual irritated yells and swear words. This time I lingered a bit to remind everyone that there was an inspection that morning. I was ignored. I didn't think much of this because by this time in our army life Wednesday inspections were generally held in contempt by all of us. At about 6.30am I was approached by Lieutenant Breedt and asked to accompany him on the morning's barracks inspection at about 7am. When the time came, Breedt, a corporal, myself and a relatively new national service 2nd lieutenant started our tour. When the time came for our bungalow to be called to order, the usual order to stand by our beds was given and we entered. What greeted our eyes was a sight that causes me to laugh out loud to this day. The consequences, however, were far from amusing... There were maybe two people standing to attention and ready for inspection. The rest, well... The two pictures that will always remain with me are of Dave Oldham (more of him soon) sitting on the edge of his unmade bed with his back to us and slowly pulling his socks on with a lit cigarette hanging out his mouth; and Ian van der Linde still fast asleep, grunting as I, and then in turn, Lieutenant Breedt tried to wake him up. "Fok off!!" was the refrain, at least twice. In desperation I leant down and said "Ian, it's inspection." He still ignored me until Breedt could stand it no more. "Van der Linde, staan op!" Hearing a different voice made up his mind, and Ian quickly stood up beside his bed in his underwear with a sheepish and bewildered look on his sleep-ridden face. The look on the officer's faces was priceless! Shock and utter disbelief best describe it. The bungalow was a mess. Almost all the beds were unmade, clothes and boots were strewn everywhere, the floor was unpolished, kases (steel cupboards) and trommels (trunks) were lying open with clothes and personal belongings hanging out. This picture was obviously the direct antithesis of what was expected for an army inspection. The lieutenant left with the rest of us in tow, pondering a response. I have to admit, as amusing as the whole scene was, even I left the place feeling somewhat shocked at the state of the tenement on such a day. I feared the worst and I wasn't going to be disappointed. Out of the entire band, I alone escaped punishment. When sentence was passed, I'm certain I was again the only one who understood the gravity of the situation. Action was taken rapidly. The boys were lined up outside the office and marched double time directly to the gymnasium, with the dreaded PTI's!!

Our company office was right next door to the gym, and as the morning progressed I watched out of my window, which faced the hall on the opposite side of the road, as the boys were sent out of the gym to run around the "Kampie" outside, and re-enter the gym. This happened about every twenty to thirty minutes. Each time the lads came out their pace was slower and fewer of them appeared. After about two hours, the ones that did appear were crawling. I saw about three or four of them vomiting, until finally the torture ended. What was left of our proud, happy cohorts was a quivering mass of humanity, barely or totally unable to walk or talk from sheer exhaustion.

I heard a commotion in the entrance of our office building and went out to see two of the roofs carrying Hugh and dropping him gently on the floor. His face was red and he threw up violently in front of me as he crawled towards me, tears of anger and resentment streaming down his face: "I swear, these people are animals, and if I ever saw any of them on the outside..." His sentence was ended by another bout of vomiting and coughing. He was sent to sick bay along with six others.

Our bungalow was a pretty unhappy place that night, and quite somber for the following two nights until our spirits gradually started lifting again. Although I'd been spared their sufferings, I felt their pain acutely—we all bled together. Alan, always a relatively quiet and soft spoken person, was almost mute for a while there. We'd been subdued... But not defeated!

THE SHAPE OF
THINGS TO COME

As the weeks wore on we became more disenchanted with playing for the PF Bring and Braais. Our bass player's behaviour was becoming increasingly erratic and unpredictable onstage, and finally a meeting was called with the captain to try and resolve these issues.

It was agreed that we would gradually hand over the Bring and Braais to the boys best suited to it, the Boeremusiek trio, while the issue of our PF bass player Des, was handed over to me to resolve because he was in my band... And so I was ordered to fire him! This was not a prospect I relished. Firstly, I was never any good at confrontations; secondly, he outranked me and was a permanent force member! Geez...

OK, so off I go to fire my superior. I decided to go just after lunch. I figured that when everyone had had something to eat they'd be in a better frame of mind.

I opened with, "Hi Des. Hope you're OK. Listen, we feel the band needs a national serviceman as a bass player to make it more authentic. Besides, we feel that the band is taking too much of a toll on your family life..." or some such BS.

He replied, "Yes, I also feel that its time I left you guys to handle things yourselves..."

I did try a more direct approach like, "Listen, you're a drunken idiot who screws up every song we play because you can't control your alcohol intake!" Which instead came out as, "Ja, listen Des, we'll miss you but you know the others feel that, like, well, it's hard you know..."

To which he replied, "Ja, but you okes must know that I've tried to keep you all on the same plak (tried to keep you all working together)".

Whatever it was, we talked in circles and both walked on eggshells, but the message got through to him that he was out. That was, however, not the last we were to hear from Des Hadlow.

Des' replacement was still a mystery, but not for long. A young guy by the name of Dave Oldham had been transferred to our company, and the captain had been told that this guy was amazing! I was walking near the duty office when the captain called me over and announced that we were taking on Dave Oldham as a bass player to replace Des. I protested. I didn't know this guy, how good he was or if he was actually a bass player.

"Oldham can play anything—he's brilliant, and, as of now he's in your band!"

Not without an audition he's not! I was ordered to take this guy on, and I did NOT like being told what to do. When I finally met him, he struck me as over-confident and somewhat opinionated. The audition was going to be tough, but not for me!

Dave walked into the practice room one Wednesday after lunch— just him, me and Pete Auths. I sat on a chair in the middle of the room, with him in front of me and Pete sitting to my left. He reached for one of the guitars:

"Hold on, what are you doing?"

"I'm going to play you one of my own songs."

"I don't want to hear one of your own songs, I want to hear how well you know our standard repertoire. Besides, we don't need a guitarist—I play guitar! Do you know this song...without the music!!! What about that song? And this...?" Poor Dave. "I see that there's very few of our songs you know. You do realise that these are standards that most musicians of any calibre should be able to perform? OK, let's see how you do on bass. Play a walking bass line, now play a running bass line... "(I had only a vague idea myself of what this should sound like). "OK, sorry. You don't pass the audition. Thank you!" Much subdued protesting from Dave.

I went back to the captain and told him I didn't think much of Oldham musically speaking, and I didn't think he would be an asset in our band.

Wrong report! "Hay, you will take him on and you will teach him the repertoire!"

I left the captain's office cursing. NOT what I wanted to hear! I didn't have a choice, and Dave Oldham joined my band. But contrary to my initial feelings, Dave was to become a team player of note and a good fit for us as a band when the resentment had subsided, but not before he'd had his say about what he felt about his initial treatment. One day, a few gigs and about four weeks after his audition, while walking with Pete and Alan to the canteen, we found ourselves also walking with a rather quiet Oldham. He was always pretty quiet, particularly during rehearsals, so I didn't think too much of it. I was in a lighthearted mood and finally felt ready to accept Dave as "one of the guys".

I greeted him with a slightly (in hindsight) patronizing "Hello there Davey." Laughs from the others—not from Oldham. I continued: "Come on there, Dave!! Pissed off with me are you?"

His response was somewhat hurtful, but also made me realize what he must have been privately going through: "I've hated every single member of this band at one time or another!!"

Surprise! Shock, even! Really? How on earth could he hate any of us? We all liked him quite a bit (as long as he didn't try and take over, of course). Slowly but surely he let each of us have a frank piece of his mind, and I realized that I must have been quite hard on him. I felt the ice slowly melting away between us, and from that day on, we were solid friends, with him taking an active and enthusiastic role in band life. In the meantime on one of our daytime excursions into town, James Thomas had introduced us to a beautiful young socialite by the name of Diane McLachlan. Her family was very wealthy and lived in a large house on Memorial road reputed to have belonged to Cecil John Rhodes. One Friday night Diane invited the band to a party she was throwing at her family's home. Most of us pitched up and Alan had invited our old Potch Girls High buddy, Diane Warner, whom I still had a little thing for. She, however, had other ideas, and I was soon going to launch myself inadvertently into the world of match making. We were all standing around on the verandah and Diane approached me and asked me who that guy was a few feet away from me. She was referring to Vincent, who was no doubt regaling Ian with another conquest story. Not being an idiot, and realising that women don't ask about a guy unless they're interested, I was hobbled and heartbroken. She then asked me to introduce her to him, which annoyed both Alan and me because, while I liked Vincent a lot, we both thought he was about as humble as a Latin Lounge Singer, with a similar dress sense, and this introduction wasn't going to do anything to quell his own opinion of himself in any way whatsoever.

I must mention here that I'm sure Vincent was aware that we found his vanity off-putting, but he was too confident to let it worry him in any way. As an observer of humanity, I knew that this side of Vince's' personality totally freaked Alan out and that he found few or no redeeming features in the man at this stage of our comradeship. For me it was a minor annoyance that I tried to ignore whenever it reared its head around me. I have other friends that met him later that felt the same way as Alan, but truth is, I saw in Vincent some substance beyond his over-inflated ego that made me value him as a friend.

As far as Diane was concerned, however disgusted (and on my part, probably somewhat jealous) we were, she was smitten. For ensuing weeks we were going to hear what an amazing guy Vincent was, what a gentleman, etc., which actually quickly cured Alan and I of any feelings of resentment, because we both figured that someone who spoke about Vincent as much as he spoke about himself probably deserved him. Ah life... It throws cold water on you, then wraps a warm towel around your head.

The end of April hove into view, bringing with it the first chills of a bitter Kimberley winter. Man, that place could get cold! One memorable night, we were booked to play at what turned out to be our final PF Bring and Braai. I wasn't prepared for the ensuing circus that was to follow.

The gig started innocently enough at around 8pm, with us launching into the usual muted first set. Eddie was on drums, Dave on bass, Pete Auths and Hugh were on keyboards and Kevin and I on guitar and vocals. Everyone was still eating, with one or two couples dancing. We got something to eat during our break, then launched into the second set. Here, things started to get interesting (and painful). About halfway through the set one of the other captains in the camp, already on his ear, came and asked us for a request. Innocent enough, you say. However, the manner of his request was to launch himself onto the stage in the middle of a song and proceed to yell in my ear in a heavy Afrikaans accent the name of the song he required. After he had yelled in my ear a few times, I managed to understand him, all the while playing guitar and trying to sing in between his drunken oral acrobatics. I told him we didn't know the song and he subsequently pulled our heads together with no regard for the laws of motion, clunking me viciously on the head, crying "Play it for fok sake!"

After recovering my senses from the blow and retreating to a safe distance I said "We can't play a song we've never heard before!"

"You can, man. It goes..." And he launched into some untuneful noise which was drowned out eventually by the band and the fact that his wife had pulled him off the stage. So much for set two!

By this time the whole place was reeling with drunk PF officers and chaos ensued as we launched into set three. It all started when, at the beginning of the set, Des Hadlow appeared at the foot of the stage, ostensibly to say hello, but actually to ask us if we would let him play. I declined. He left, but as we continued our set he kept on asking, and of course when the other officers and NCO's heard him ask, they all joined the chorus. Without waiting for permission he jostled onto the stage, and entreated me further. Against my much better judgement, and under the intimidating eyes of the other officers, I conceded defeat and asked Dave Oldham to lend Des his bass. I was not happy being hobbled in mid set like this, but felt I had very little choice but to indulge him. There was one problem—Des was seriously drunk and the first song we played we had to stop halfway through. He had wet himself! Smelling of urine and determined to continued, we launched into "(How Much Is) That Doggy in the Window". At that very moment, Vincent, Nick Vlok and Ian, who had been out on the town, entered stage right, looking very civilian in their mufti. Their look of amusement said it all. I started mock-singing the song, playing the most jarring chords, singing out of time, all the while killing myself laughing while trying to sing. I unhooked my axe and slipped backstage as the song progressed, as did the rest of the band except for dear old Pete Auths who was always trying to do the right thing. Des was falling about the stage in a drunken stupor. Pete was ducking behind the organ as the neck of the bass guitar swung dangerously around past his face. Interestingly enough Des was aware that we'd all left and he kept on turning around, becoming very pissed off and agitated as he called out for yours truly. Ian jumped out and hooked my guitar up and started imitating Des, at which point the latter got extremely angry and aggressive and started chasing Ian around the stage, the two of them like a pair of ducks fighting, with Des drunkenly running and falling after Ian, who was making seriously funny protest noises, rather like an annoyed hen being chased by an amorous rooster around a farmyard. The evening came to an end when Des went crashing off the stage, bass guitar and all, and was finally lifted up by his PF buddies and helped out of the hall.

I stood in the wings watching this circus with disbelief, amusement and a strange sense of power. This was outside army working hours, and oddly, the same rules seemed to not apply in this situation. There was an opinion beginning to take shape in the minds of the officers that this band was slightly above the rule of law in this camp. Were they beginning to feel, dare I say it, begrudgingly beholden to us by the fact that we were not the run of the mill national servicemen, and we were supplying a service that they rather enjoyed? We were just having fun, but they enjoyed the music and, in a strange way, recognised our talent and the fact that we were so tight as comrades. We finished our set and said goodnight. I can't remember exactly how that evening ended, but I do know that that was the last time we ever did a PF Bring and Braai.

STAYING ALIVE

A round the beginning of May we became privy to a Battle of the Bands competition taking place on the 31st of that month—Republic Day. This was made known to me by Vincent, Hugh and Ian, who had somehow befriended a rather slimy and sexually suspect character by the name of Koort Wessels, who had an equally slimy friend whose name escapes me. Koort had organised the competition and knew of our band through Hugh, who seemed particularly friendly with the two of them. We were invited to enter the contest.

The captain was about to embark on some kind of training course for about six weeks, but we got the go ahead to enter. Things were about to get interesting. Vincent and I both decided that our best chance of getting anywhere in this contest was to combine forces, which we duly did, and rehearsals started in earnest. A few days into our rehearsals, and just before he took off for his course, the captain took about eight of us into town with him to have a farewell lunch. While heading down one of Kimberley's main thoroughfares we passed a music shop in which was sitting a beautiful Fender Rhodes suitcase model piano. We went inside and Vincent sat down at it with the captain and all of us looking on, and he played a few bars and started cooing and aahing over it.

"Do you want it?" the captain asked.

"Aah, seriously?" replied Vincent.

"Yes—I'll authorise it for you," reiterated the captain.

"Aah yes please, Captain!! Thanks so much!!" replied a grateful Vincent Du Chenne.

Fatherly, very fond grin... And one new keyboard gets added to our arsenal.

Now here's where I grudgingly give Vincent credit for foresight and direction. At our first rehearsal, one of the first things we discussed was repertoire for the competition, and Vincent pulled out a tape of the very recently released *Saturday Night Fever* album.

"If we do this, guys, we'll win! Chicks love this stuff!" said Vincent knowingly. I'm generally suspicious of new songs, and at this stage of my musical development, particularly suspicious of, and revolted by, disco music. But so much on the album was by the Bee Gees, a band we all knew but were all surprised to see rear their heads again. So we set about listening to the material, working out chords and deciphering lyrics, which was always a difficult undertaking, but one we took very seriously, I particularly, because I prided myself in getting the right words down. I was generally somewhat a cut above the others in this regard, but even I slipped up on some occasions, only to find out YEARS later that I'd been singing the wrong words of a particular line of the song "Stayin' Alive"—"I've got the wings of heaven on my shoes" was interpreted by me as "When I wake up in my long lost shoes". A line from the song "Baby Come Back"— "All day long, wearing a mask of false bravado"—became "All day long, wearing a mascots false bravado" etc. As far as chords were concerned, well, we didn't get them all right but we got them close enough to impress upon people that we knew what we were doing and a bit more. That first rehearsal, and subsequent ones, have long abided in my memory. We really all had a sense of purpose and doing something new fuelled that sense. What's more, we sounded pretty powerful. We had a line-up of two drummers (Eddie and Nick), three guitarists (myself, Ian and Kevin), one bass player (Dave—does a band ever need more?), three keyboards (Pete, Hugh and Vincent) and three brass guys (Alan, James and Willie). The vocal duties were left mainly to Vincent and me, with the other vocalists, Dave and Kevin, doing harmonies. Vincent chose songs he thought the chicks would go mad for—"How Deep is Your Love" and "More Than a

Woman", while I was left to tackle "Staying Alive", "Night Fever" and "Disco Inferno".

We were invincible, and we knew it. The troops would line up outside our practice room window to watch us rehearse, and we would give them a show. Lots of chiefs in the rehearsal room and only a few Indians... Egos flying everywhere—especially since we had an audience! We did get the work done, though, and by the time the 31st rolled around, we were ready... On the afternoon of the event we set out with all our equipment for the hosting venue, which was the Kimberley Agricultural Showgrounds on the outskirts of town. Behind the main arena was a function hall where the competition was going to be held. After trekking our gear in there, we set up and did a sound check. Although the stage was a good size, we had to share it with a couple of the other acts, so it was a bit of a squeeze, but not uncomfortable.

We packed up the walkables (guitars, mics and the like) and headed back to camp for an early supper. Vincent had a car, so he, Hugh, Ian and Nick climbed in and headed off for the venue at about 7pm. The rest of us followed in a Bedford truck that we'd commissioned from the Transport Park. The place was abuzz when we arrived. Half of Kimberley had turned up to see the competition, so we were filled with the typical nervous excitement that goes with these events. All in all there were about five bands participating. Did we stand a chance? At this point I wasn't so sure. We hadn't heard the other acts, so we had no frame of reference, and bigger ain't necessarily better. The first band got on stage and tuned up and after being introduced by Koort, resplendent in his black bell bottoms, frilly dress shirt and shoes, slicked back black hair and heavily rimmed glasses, they launched into their first song. A Boeremusiek quartet. Now I was really worried! The dance floor filled up so quickly it made our heads spin. The band played about a half hour set, put down their instruments and headed off the stage. We got on... After our initial afternoon set-up, getting ourselves organised on stage was a somewhat haphazard and rigorous affair. Between the lot of us we must have set up and sound checked in about half an hour. We were all feeding off each other's nervousness—it was magnificent, exciting and paranoia-inducing! I always panic during a sound-check. I want to check a thousand things at the same time, and you never know if you're loud enough in comparison to your drummer, or in our case, drummers! With Eddie, you had someone who could rival John Bonham (look him up!) for loudness, and with Nick, someone who would be quite at home playing in a jazz trio in a small cafe. Tonight, however, adrenalin kicked in for everyone, including Nick. I never saw him play with such energy before or after that night. What a spectacle we were, but a spectacle with a sense of purpose. We finished our sound-check, and the train pulled out of the station... I don't remember the order of the songs. I do remember blowing any competition we had completely out of the room! The stunned and completely amazed looks we got for doing the *Saturday Night Fever* repertoire, followed by the floor being filled to breaking point, filled us with a total sense of justification in our mission, and as I looked around I saw that look of satisfaction on the whole band's faces, as if the twelve of us had all planned and constructed the Taj Mahal together that very night. I remember singing my three SNF songs, among others, and Vincent doing his, both of us as if in slow motion. What a night!

And then I saw her... My heart stopped, then started again as a flush crossed my face. There she was, dancing in the middle of the floor, her long blonde hair shining as if a spotlight had been trained on her alone! I was transfixed, but sang with renewed vigour, hoping to catch her eye. To no avail. I had to find out who she was. Now, I had not been seriously involved with any girls for about eighteen months. I had decided that the wise thing to do before entering the army was to avoid any emotional involvement, and only date casually. The wisdom of this decision was borne out by the number of "Dear John" letters that other guys of my intake received, and the helpless anguish and heartache that followed. As I watched this siren on the dance floor, we finished to huge applause and shouts for encores. We did two more songs and then hopped off the stage in triumph, leaving Koort to sing our praises as I headed straight for her table.

She was sitting with an older woman, who turned out to be her mother. I turned on my peculiar brand of charm. Not smarmy or complementary, just what I called my "nice guy" approach. Mother was smitten with me; my amore was indifferent. I kept my cool and asked questions, and discovered that her name was Sandra Leonard and her mom was Phyllis. She had blue eyes that I could drown in, and I was totally in love! She had an air of mystery about her that left me feeling like someone struggling to finish a crossword puzzle! I was to experience this feeling a lot during the next six months... I asked whether I could get her phone number—mother gave it to me before I could finish the sentence—after which I enquired as to when it would be possible to see her again. With a smile, mother said "Phone her!" Sandra was actually somewhat embarrassed that her mother was arranging her love-life for her, which I found quite amusing, but I was left under no false impression that this girl was a pushover—anything but! They got up to leave. I said goodbye and that I would phone. I was walking on a cloud... The next band got on—some youngsters from Kimberley Boys High. Little did I know that the keyboard player, Tony Drake, and his family were going to become life-long friends. When they launched into their first few songs, Ian and I cast an eye over them with the light-hearted air of unannounced victors who had nothing more to prove. We watched the guitarist in particular, who was still learning his chops, and chuckled to ourselves as he faked some fast lead runs. We went to the bar to get a beer then went over to the others and sat down and talked and told jokes. About three quarters of an hour later, Koort clambered up onto the stage. We held our breath—we knew he was going to announce the winners. Tony's band was announced as the runners-up. "And the winner is... Magirus, from 1 Maintenance Unit". We went ballistic, jumped up and went forward to accept our prize. I don't even remember what we won; we were just so rapt at winning. And in fact, even though we were unaware at that moment, the biggest prize was not winning the competition, but what it did for our standing on the local gig scene.

SIPPING THE NIGHT
FANTASTIQUE

s I said in the previous chapter, we were blissfully unaware
that our status was going to change from an army band
playing for the PF's, to a bona fide gig band in our own right.
As far as we were concerned, we'd just won a competition. We had
no idea that the people who had seen us perform that night were
going to be asking us to do just about every gig in town.

It all started innocently enough with Hugh and I sitting in the
duty office about five days after our triumph. Someone had phoned
the base enquiring after us, and the call was put through directly to
our office. The captain was still on his course and would be for the
next few weeks. We had an NSM lieutenant in charge of us who was
totally on our level, so as a result, Hugh and I had, for all intents and
purposes, the run of the place.

"Transport 1:1, Private Hay speaking."

Heavy Afrikaans accent on the other end. "Hello, ya, we are
having a dance this Saturday, and I was wondering whether we could
book the band? I know we is taking a chance—you guys must be very
busy."

"Actually, we've had a cancellation this Saturday [lies] and we
happen to be free, so we can do it."

"Ag, fantastic man!! What do you guys charge?"

Long pause. "Um, er..." This was the first time we'd been asked
that question. "R150 for four forty five minute sets.".

"Great! Can we book you?"

"Sure. Please give us your address and starting time."

Wow! A paying gig!? Hugh and I were both excited, but flummoxed. How were we going to get there? What kind of permission did we need? Who did we ASK for permission?—the captain wasn't around! We had to think fast, so we went to our NSM loot and asked him. He cleared it with the major and we were good to go. The second problem of transport was cleared when we realised that we were part of the transport division and had the power to requisition vehicles from the vehicle pool for the whole camp. That Saturday we got ourselves a Bedford truck, loaded it up with our gear, and after showering and getting dressed, we were on our way.

The gig went off without a hitch and we got back about 1am. As it was Sunday the following day, we could sleep in a bit at least, which we happily did.

On the Monday, we had work to do! Hugh and I sat down and worked out how we were going to present our services to our prospective clients. After some discussion we agreed to offer the following services: For both bands combined we stuck with the R150 fee; for my seven piece band we charged R120; for Vincent's five piece we charged R100; and for a small combo of three, or the boereorkes, we charged R90. Very pleased with this outcome, we informed the others, who seemed quite happy with this arrangement. The camp's 2IC, Major Ferreira was then informed and it was decided, somewhat to our dismay, that half the proceeds for each gig would be kept in a slush fund by the camp. We expected to not see this money again. I was wrong...

Actually, life in our office without the captain around was very pleasant. We had pretty much the run of everything, and soon got used to being in a fair position of authority. Peachy!! In fact, we got so used to calling the shots and running the show that when the captain returned I was at the forefront of his wrath and his bid to restamp his authority. Until he returned, however, we were almost a law unto ourselves.

In the meantime, I was trying to kick-start my romantic life. I was happily single until the night I met Sandra—now I wanted to be un-single. That first phone call is always nerve wracking. Mother was only too happy to hand the phone to her..."It's Clive... From Magirus... The army band, man!"

Sandra: "Hello?!"

My heart was in my mouth. "Hi, Sandra, it's Clive. How are you?"

And so on. Mystery girl, this one. I could never read her. I was hooked! I managed to wangle a visit on the Wednesday night. I was so nervous I decided to take Kevin with me for moral support, and because he had access to a vehicle and had an army drivers license! Number thirteen Ilva road was our destination. Unlucky for some? We'd have to see. After a journey of about fifteen minutes, and a few twists and turns, we arrived. The time was about 7.30pm. We went through the gate and approached the door like we were going to the principal's office! Knocking...or was that my knees? Mother came to the door with a big grin on her face. We went in and there she was, standing between the entrance and the lounge, white short-sleeve blouse, blue jeans and white sandals. Breast length blonde hair, and those blue eyes.

Seated on a comfortable looking chair was her father, Lyell senior, and on the couch was Lyell junior. They were both watching TV, so we quickly introduced ourselves and shook hands. Dad was about 5ft 4, with a calm, quiet, but friendly exterior. Very unassuming. I immediately felt at ease. Lyell junior had a similar demeanour, but with a slightly cheeky and sardonic take on everything. He was the youngest. Sandra had an older brother, Anthony, who was in the Air Force in Pretoria. Mom hustled off to the kitchen to organise eats and drinks, and the small talk started:

"So where are you from?"

"Joburg; Kempton Park actually, on the East Rand."

"And you Kevin?"

Kevin? Hey what about me? Slight pangs of jealousy. Did she actually fancy Kevin? Control, control! No emotion! Wait until you get asked something again. Change of tactic—talk to parents—win them over! "What do you do Mr. Leonard?"

"I'm an electrician..."

"Oh, great! Must be interesting, and slightly dangerous, working with electricity and electrical stuff..."

"Ya, it's just a job though."

Mom came through with the eats and drinks. We thanked her and tucked in. I snuck a look at Sandy. She was sitting with her legs tucked together on the chair, looking down. She was gorgeous, but there was still that air of indifference that I couldn't seem to break through. She didn't seem bored, but I did not seem to be making an impression at all. The evening wore on for about another hour, with us intermittently talking and watching the TV... Well, I wasn't watching much. After all this time, I'm trying to remember how I felt that night. Mother made us feel so welcome, interesting and liked, it was almost like we could not really put a foot wrong. The message didn't seem to be getting through to Sandy! Kevin and I decided that we'd better be getting back to the camp before someone missed us. We got up, thanked mother again for the eats and headed for the door. Sandy walked us out. I was in despair and frustration. I so wanted to grab her and kiss her, but I knew that any reckless moves would kill any chances I might have. I just turned around at the gate, asked her if we could come again sometime.

"Sure. Bye now."

"Bye."

We got into the vehicle and off we went.

As the weeks progressed, every time before a phone call, every hour before a visit, all seemed like a Dali painting. The visits came and went, and still no positive signals. I was beginning to despair, and had almost resigned myself to the possibility that this romance might not be written. I took along friends that I didn't perceive as such a threat in order to boost my chances, but it seemed like a lost cause. And then, one night, when I'd written off my chances, I went visiting Sandy with Dave Oldham as my sidekick. We had a good evening and I was feeling stronger and not so unsure of myself. At the end of the evening Sandy, Dave and I walked out to the car. Dave said goodnight and got in the car. I turned to say goodnight and wondered, as I glanced into those blue eyes, whether I saw a faint glimmer of something different. Something small, but it was definitely there... Or was I fooling myself? I decided that I was going to act. Whatever happened, it didn't matter anymore. If I wound up with egg on my face, I could deal with it! I said "Bye", and as I did so, I leant down and put my lips to hers. No resistance. I gently opened my mouth... Still no resistance. I searched out her tongue and found it. The sweetest, longest kiss followed, and we were swept up into each other at that moment. I knew she was mine. We unlocked from our embrace and parted ways.

As I climbed into the car, Oldham turned and looked at me and exclaimed "Man, you've got stars in your eyes!"

STARS INDEED

Stars Indeed! That was the start of a five month romance that had been brewing, in my mind at least, for some time. It was also the build up and continuation of our local success as a band in Kimberley. Nothing and no-one could touch us. We were just about a law unto ourselves (at least 'til the captain got back), and we were left to our own devices. The bookings were flowing in and we were the toast of the town. On top of everything, we had the power of the government behind us, which gave us an almost invincible aura in the eyes of the public (and in our own eyes!). As I mentioned earlier, there was a certain amount of resentment that we had to deal with, particularly from some of the officers and PF's, but on the whole, we were riding the wave.

On the romance front, those first three months with Sandy were incredible. I was bowled over. Here was a girl who really kept me on my toes! I was tossed about the ocean of love like a buoy ('scuse the pun) in a storm—but I was loving every minute of it. Any excuse to snog we jumped at. Phyllis (mom) loved me and treated me like a king. Every time I visited we were sequestered in Sandra's room by her, where, between snogs, we would discuss life, the future, the present, love and anything in between, all the while being waited on by Phyllis, which in hindsight was her way of keeping a discreet eye on us. Interestingly, ours was not an overtly sexual relationship. We LOVED kissing each other, but I could never fathom her true feelings for me, and more than anything, that kept me totally intrigued and somewhat shy and confused as to whether I could explore her further. I would later discover that exploration was highly desired, but at the time it felt like that would be a step overboard from which

I would never be rescued, and I was quite happy with the status of my love boat. I spent most of my weekends at her house and if we weren't playing I'd sleep over. We'd go shopping in town on Saturday mornings, go back to her place in the afternoon, sit on the couch in each other's arms and watch TV, talk, kiss, eat, drink, argue, kiss again... You get the picture!

Vincent and Ian took a very patronising view of our relationship, and would occasionally take the piss. I didn't particularly mind. Vincent's relationship with Diane kept him at her place exclusively whenever he visited her—he never dared venture out with her for some reason, and Ian was not seeing anyone in Kimberley at that stage. I suspect there was this attitude on their part, of "How the heck did HE wind up with HER?" And their answer was to try and make light of us. Did it matter? Not really—I was in my element, surrounded by the girl I was crazy about and her doting family.

By the end of July, however, things at camp were about to change! June had seen me stand my last official beat. Although I was a company clerk and well ensconced in my company duties, the band was called upon to stand guard at the airport one cold June night. This kind of thing sometimes happened just before a new intake, when the numbers at camp had dwindled due to people being posted to other camps and people going on course or border duty. That night they had run out of people and so I was called upon. I had hardly stood beat at all since March, so this was a hard pill to swallow. I'll never forget it, and I vowed that this would be the last time! The venue was Kimberley Airport near my old hunting ground, the Transport Park. I was given the worst draw—8-10pm/2-4pm. Being June, the night was bitterly cold, and I remember when I finished my beat, going back to the guard tent and sleeping the last two hours in all my clothes, including my great coat, and being covered with six blankets. I was warm, though. I remember seeing the Roofs arrive that morning as I went off to breakfast. They were in shock with the temperature being easily in the minus degrees, and they had that forlorn and confused look on their faces that must have been so obvious to the army personnel and troops when we first arrived! I was suddenly aware that I'd been in the army for one whole year—half of the time required of me by the state! I was now an Ou Man (Old Man—army term for national servicemen who had completed nine months or more) in the true sense of the expression, and I relished my position, reflecting on the past year and how it had turned out, with great satisfaction.

I was, however, in for a surprise that July. Things were changing quickly and I wasn't so sure that I liked some of the changes! Firstly, the captain had returned and had bitten my head off on the first day, as previously described, but once he'd re-established (in his mind) his position as the head of the pack in the office, things settled quickly back to normal. The one thing that bothered me initially was his reaction to our pricing, which he insisted we change, as he said we were charging too much. Hugh and I persuaded him otherwise, though, and continued charging what, in retrospect, were very reasonable prices. Another development occurred which I was actually quite happy with; Hugh and I were promoted to Lance Corporal, an event that preceded a barrage of abuse directed at me from Kaffertjie de Meyer when he found out. "Wie was so laf om vir HOM 'n streep te gee!!??" (Who was the idiot who promoted HIM?). I took the comment from where it came. The promotion came with the privilege of eating in the NCO's mess—it had marginally better food and was less crowded—being respectfully acknowledged by the lower ranking privates who saluted non-coms in the form of a "Strek", and a huge pay rise of approximately R10 per month!

The one change, however, that ruffled my feathers in a big way was a piece of news that made me pull up my guard and put me on alert indefinitely.

I can't remember who it was, but someone informed me that Major Ferreira had requested that John Ferrier be returned to our camp from border duty, and that he was taking over one of the bands!

Freaked out does not even begin to describe my feelings. I was indignant, confused, angry, felt that my authority was about to be eroded beyond repair... The emotions ran wild. We'll see about that! I went to the captain to verify the story. Yes, it was true! John was arriving within the week, and he was to be incorporated into one of the bands! I told the captain that I had too many personnel, and that he would be a better fit for Vincent's band! The matter hung in the balance while the days rolled by... Before he arrived, I warned every one of my band members that if they spoke to John Ferrier, they would incur my wrath. I didn't want to give him the slightest hint that he might be welcome in my group. Luckily for me, Vincent, Ian and the rest of Vincent's band had not experienced Mr. Bombastic. John was about as subtle as a steamroller, and I still had memories of him trying to edge me and anyone else who was playing a guitar right out of the picture. Was I worried? You betcha!! I was still mastering my craft and the last thing I needed then was for someone to come and push me out the way, no matter how good they were. He was, after all, a better lead player than me, and that wouldn't do!

His leadership skills, however, were highly questionable, and he had a way of pissing people off within a very short space of time. He wasn't an aggressive individual, though. He possessed the finer traits of the artistic temperament and was fairly articulate, and on the whole not unlikeable, and interesting to converse with. But there were the constant "I know better" interruptions, and the fact that he pushed so many people's buttons...(By the way, I rank him today as one of my very best friends).

The end of the week arrived. I successfully made every effort to avoid John, for the meantime anyway, and I managed to persuade the captain that John would be much better utilised in Vincent's band—and besides, I'd worked with him before and I didn't want him anywhere near my group! It was with some satisfaction, therefore, that I witnessed from a safe distance, John's first rehearsal with Vincent's band... They had no idea what they were in for! I still continued avoiding him, however, more for fear of being engaged in a one-way conversation than anything else. I managed to keep this up for just over a month, until one day walking to the canteen with Oldham and Pete Auths, John happened to pass us.

(John): "Hi Clive."

I walked on.

"Hi Pete".

(Soto voce) "Hi John ..."

(Me) " Shut up, Pete! Don't talk to him!" We walked on towards the canteen.

John, obviously confused and insulted, followed hard on our heels. Turning in front of me he stopped me. "What the hell's wrong with you Clive Hay?? You haven't even had the courtesy to greet me in all the time I've been here!!"

"Don't play dumb with me," I said, "you're not getting a foot in my band. Think you can just walk in and take over? We've worked our asses off to get this band up and running and if you want to be a part of any band you're going to have to learn to have a little humility!!"

"What the heck are you talking about? I was just ordered by the major to return here because he thought I'd be needed for duty in one of the bands!!"

"Well, we were informed in no uncertain terms that you were coming to take over one of the bands! And that's not going to happen! I mean, how would you react if you were told that? And I know you John Ferrier. Any opportunity to take over!"

" Clive, I swear I don't know anything about that."

"Really?"

"Yes! I swear!"

...

"Well... Anyway, how's it going with Vincent?..."

And so, a friendship was renewed and misunderstandings cleared up. Later on in months when I chatted to him about the incident and we laughed together, I asked him again: "Were you really prepared to just take a back seat?"

"Well, would you, Clive? You're just as ambitious as I am! Don't tell me that if you were in my position you wouldn't want to sneak in and then start exerting your influence!" "I guess you're right. But I wasn't going to let it happen in my band!" We chuckled wryly.

THE KICK INSIDE

So on we went. I still made an effort to do as many gigs as possible using only my personnel but it didn't always work out that way. Sometime toward the end of August, when the final frosts of winter were doing their best to denude what was left of the almost semi desert surrounding Kimberley, I did my first gig with Ferrier. We were booked to do a dance in Jan Kempdorp, a small military town some hundred kilometres north of Kimberley. This time, however, they wanted the whole shooting match—both bands playing at full tilt! That Friday afternoon we loaded the Bedford and moved out. I sat in front with Eddie, who was driving, and Dave Oldham. James, Pete, Hugh, John and Alan sat in the back with the gear. The others all went in Vincent and Ian's cars. I have to say that Eddie was a great driver, so I was happy to be up front. I didn't have my driver's license at that point, and both John and Eddie had their army Bedford licenses. Eddie... I'd never met someone who got so worried about the smallest things. He was almost always worried about getting caught doing something that most of us took for granted was deliberately overlooked by our masters. And he was worried that we weren't worried. We almost always argued. When he was behind a wheel or a drum kit, however, he was an entirely different animal—relaxed, convivial, in control. I think that that was it—unless he was doing these things, he felt that everything might get away from him. He was like a guy running after a bus and only just making it, but when he got on the bus he was most comfortable in the driver's seat! He had a good heart, however, and proved to be a good backstop for those of us who were AWOL-ing.

This day, then, he was in control, driving us to our destination. The three of us chatted inanely, with the excitement that comes from discovering a new journey and town, knowing that we were going to do what we loved best, and still get paid for it! We got to the venue and set up. Being a gig for the local military installation, Vincent and I went and spoke to the officer in charge to find out the fine dining and fiscal arrangements. After eating, we climbed on stage and kicked off.

The first set was typically laid back, but from the second set onwards, things started to get a bit prickly—for me, anyway. I was trying my best to be magnanimous in the presence of Mr. Bombastic. It was hard not to be on the defensive, particularly when it came to solos. I was always under the impression that John viewed every gig as his opportunity to show off, and because of his size I had no choice but to reluctantly get in on the act, even if I felt it wasn't the appropriate song or time. We took a break and sat down. John launched into some philosophical observation, something along the lines of, "If a tree falls in a forest with no one around, does it make a noise?" Whatever it was, he was a great conversationalist, and I did enjoy hearing a lot of what he had to say.

We used to laugh because he always had a theory about something—rather like the character Ann Elk from the Monty Python team skit. Monty Python... We were ALWAYS quoting the Pythons. When we first started socialising in Kimberley, in the days of Des Hadlow, we would often hang out with the De Lange family whom Ian and Huey had befriended and then introduced me to. I remember sitting around a few times with their daughters at one of the local hotels (before the Kimberley Hotel became our big hangout), with Alan quipping away with the "Sheep sketch" and many others, and all of us falling about laughing. The youngest daughter Karen, I was told, had a thing for me at the time. I wasn't that interested due to her age, mainly—she was still a fairly young school girl. Months later, Vincent took great delight in swearing me to secrecy about the fact that he was cheating on Diane with her. I'm not sure why, but I was destined to become a target of confidentiality regarding many of my colleagues trysts. I have my theories, which I shall cover later.

Back at the gig, we had finished for the night and were facing the tortuous drive back to camp, then unloading before finally getting some sleep. I hated unloading. P.A.s, drums, amps, keyboards, guitars, the organ, the enormously heavy Leslie speaker (which, by the way, my guitar sounded fantastic through) and all the other little crapola, like mics and cables. When we arrived at the camp it was close to 2am and I was exhausted. I just wanted to go to sleep and unload in the morning, but James, bless his heart, encouraged me to get it all out of the way before we hit the sack.

I'm constantly reminded that in life we have periods of intimacy with people. I'm not just talking about physical intimacy, but friendship, camaraderie, closeness. I'm obviously more aware of this with women, as the intimacy takes on a sensual dimension, which seems to enhance this feeling tenfold. These intense periods with women are often all too brief, particularly in our youth, where they tend to slip through our fingers as we navigate our way through love's oceans in search of our final romantic destination. One of my fondest memories during my time with Sandy was a trip out to Warrenton one Saturday with her parents. Warrenton was a pretty little town next to the Vaal river, about thirty to fifty kilometres from Kimberley, bordering the old Transvaal province, and the Cape province. We had lunch there and then sat against the car. Sandy was sitting on the bonnet behind me with her arms draped around my neck, and whispering sweet things in my ear. I felt like an absolute king! We moved off from the car and started talking about our lives and what we expected from them. Being the enigma that she was, when I asked Sandy what kind of future she envisaged for herself, her answer was surprising.

"I guess I'll just settle in Kimberley, get married and raise a family..."

Settle in Kimberley?? "Really?" I replied. "Come on! Don't you want to do something special with your life?"

"Well, what do you want to do?" she asked in a slightly defensive manner.

"Are you kidding?" I replied again. "There's a whole world out there! I want to travel! I want to go to Europe! I want to hit the big time with my music!! Don't you want to see the world??"

"No. I'm quite happy just to stay here. You're very ambitious, Clive!"

I did wonder a bit whether I featured at all in her plan, but I didn't dwell on it long at all, mainly because I suddenly realised that I had a vision for my life. Regardless, I was with my mystery girl, and my life was content there and then!

However, as is my usual routine with women, paradise was about to be crapped on. Sandy and I had the usual lovers' tiffs, but one weekend proved to be something of an enigma. On a Saturday morning (again), we were doing the rounds in town—shopping, getting a bite at the local Spur restaurant, window shopping and the like—when we passed by a record store. A few days earlier, Kate Bush had made her South African television debut with "Wuthering Heights", which I had sadly missed. Sandy and her mom had given me such a descriptive run down on the video that I was really sorry I missed it! Needless to say, I loved the song, so when we passed the record store and I saw her debut album *The Kick Inside* sitting in the window, I had to buy it for my sweetheart. The album cover was quite distinctive, with a raven- haired seventeen year old Kate hanging resplendently from some wooden structure next to an enormous eye. She was as enigmatic to observe as her songs were to listen to.

We played the album the whole afternoon, absorbing all the songs both lyrically and musically. Sandy and I sat cuddled together on the couch, with her staring intently at the album cover... I thought nothing of it. I was staying over at the Leonards that night, so I'd brought my necessities with me for the stay. We had dinner, watched a movie and then went to bed. I always used Anthony's room. He was in the Air Force and I'd only met him once, but he was just like the rest of the family—friendly and polite, if not a little more intense than the rest of them. Right now he was in Pretoria and I was the son-in-stead. The next morning, Mrs. woke me with breakfast in bed, and there was my girl, come to say hello. Things were a little different, however. More stand-offish, not as loving. Something was wrong! I had a shower and we went out for a walk and returned. Still no change. Couch time! I asked her what was wrong. No reply. I repeated the question.

This time the answer was, "Nothing!"

Yeah, right! Try as I might, however, I could get nothing out of her—just a stubborn, dismissive silence. Not even anger, and believe me, she could get angry. On one occasion as her mom was driving me back to camp, the sarcasm was flowing so hard toward me that even Mrs. finally turned around and yelled "Sandra, stop being a complete bitch!"

The rest of that morning I tried to get an answer out of her and was stonewalled at almost every turn. After lunch I still persisted, and finally started making some headway. A little more gentle prodding, and out it came:

"I dreamt about you last night." ... OK, not so bad... "I dreamt that you were with another girl..."

OK, some sensitivity required... "So all this agony was about a dream??" I asked, being as sensitive but as matter-of-fact as I could.

"Yes. The girl had long black hair... It was very real to me!" she said.

I glanced over at the Kate Bush album cover—long black hair! I grabbed the album cover: "The girl didn't look like THIS by any chance, did she?" I asked.

Silence. Busy perusing the cover.

I continued: "You were looking at this thing the whole afternoon yesterday. No wonder you're having dreams about women with long black hair! I'm crazy about you—I don't know ANY women with long black hair!" Problem solved, mind at rest, back to osculating again! I thought no more of this incident for the next two months... Earlier that same July when the captain had returned along with John Ferrier, a few young lieutenants fresh off the officers course in Pretoria had joined our ranks. One of them, who seemed to take a particular interest in me, maybe because I was so flippant in my interactions with the other NSM officers, was a very nice guy by the name of Mike Coote. On our first meeting he asked me what my name was. I was slightly worried, with him being an officer, and thought I was in trouble for a minute. The reason for his interest in me soon became apparent, however, when he asked me if I knew of any nice girls in town. Looking at him with opportunistic eyes and being constantly short of transport to Sandy, I asked him if he had a car. Affirmative!

"Well, my girlfriend lives in town, and I need to see her occasionally. If I fix you up, are you OK to take me there from time to time?"

"Absolutely!"

We had an instant friendship, and I had an instant alternative means of transport.

Sizing him up, and being satisfied that this was a pretty decent bloke, I could think of one girl who would be perfect for him—Diane McLachlan! When I phoned her she was very gracious but somewhat sceptical, and only agreed to go out with Mike on condition that she vet him first. That Thursday, Mike and I paid a visit to Diane in her parents' stately home and my instincts proved right. They hit it off immediately and a double date was set with the two of them and Sandy and myself for that Friday, for dinner and a drive-in movie to see, of all things, *Grease* starring John Travolta as Danny, and Olivia Newton John as SANDY! Wow, was I a matchmaker or what! First Vincent and Diane, now Mike and Diane. More than I knew, because about two years later Mike and Diane were married, and Vincent and Diane stayed together for ten years before calling it quits. My matchmaking skills were to surface again in the near future...

In the meantime, I was to become a somewhat reluctant co-singer to a fairly well known South African singer by the name of Caroline (a name that was to feature largely in my future) Du Preez. Caroline was invited to do a cabaret with our band for the PF's. Vincent had organised this with the captain through the Don Hughes Organisation, an entertainment agency based in Johannesburg, for the purposes of giving the troops and PFs some first class female entertainment.

Caroline was gotten from the airport with much fanfare by Vincent, the captain, myself and a few others. She was a somewhat buxom, fairly sexy thirty-something lady, who was slightly on the pleasantly plump side! Needless to say, when she landed, the egos took off, with Vincent and the Cap making sure they were her principal escorts to the camp. With the popularity of the movie *Grease*, everyone was singing the songs, so besides all members of both our teams being Caroline's backing band, I was opted in to be Danny to her Sandy for "You're the One That I Want." Now people, put me onstage with a guitar and call me Clapton, I'm that confident. Put me onstage with only a mic and I'm like Big Bird with a bad back. Not only was I embarrassed at doing sexy interactions with our leading lady, I couldn't help but think that I would be much happier doing this with my own Sandy. Not only that, but the song was slightly higher than I could reach vocally, and the scornful and derisive stares of my PF enemies made my confidence in doing the number slide off the meter. Nevertheless, I got through the number OK, and Caroline went back to Joburg, job done.

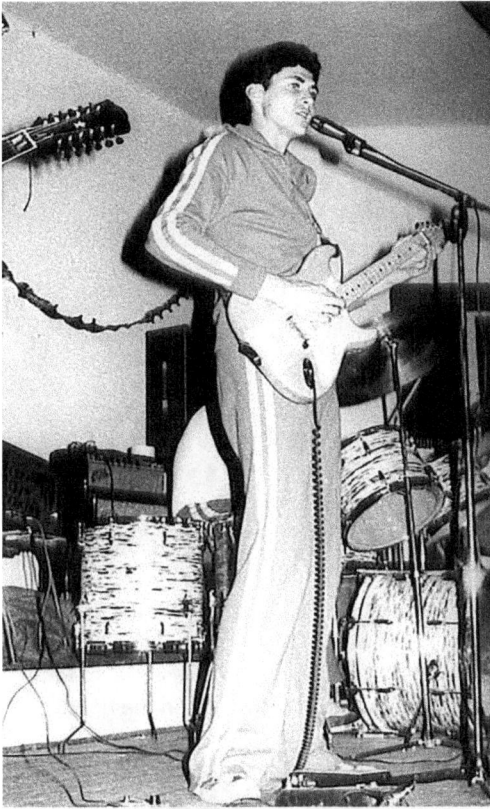

Yours truly performing in the camp's hall with Stratocaster copy. Note the Magirus tracksuit – much better looking black and white.

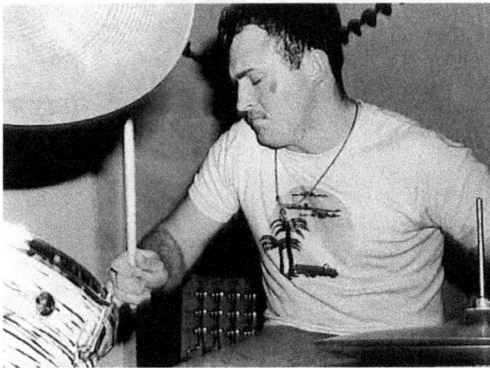

Eddie, our erstwhile drummer.

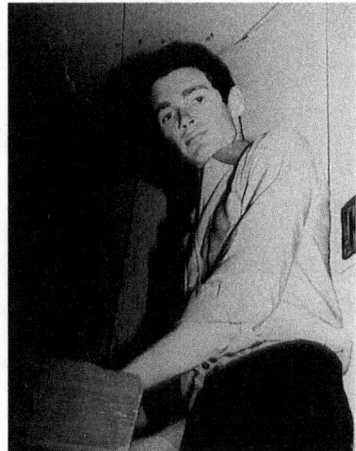

Hugh – Vincent's organist and my partner-in-crime in the company HQ.

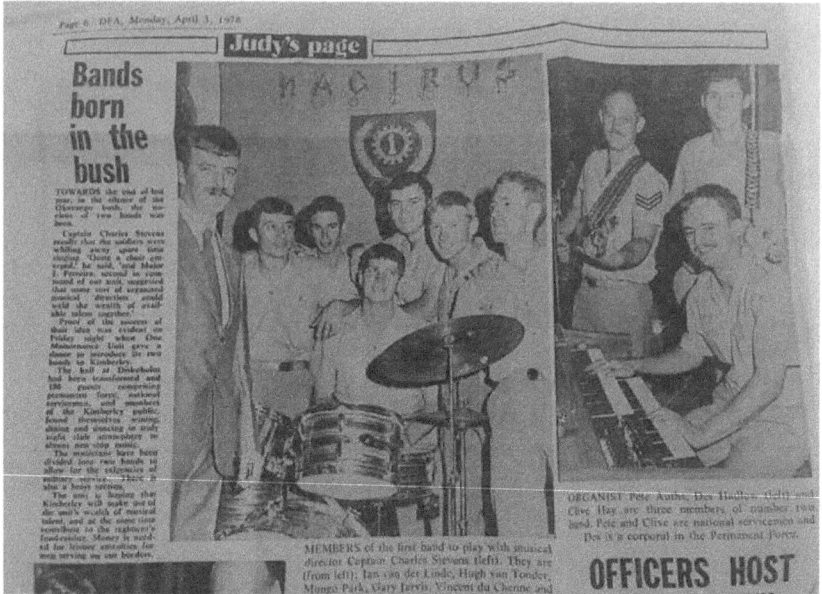

The infamous Diamond Fields Advertiser article, relegating my band to the "number two band"! Vincent's original lineup was shown in the photo on the left with the Cat (Captain Stevens), while I'm standing with our bass player PF Corporal Des Hadlow behind a seated Pete Auths in the photo on the right.

The eternally loveable Pete 'Duck' Auths.

Dave and I having a quick discussion about the next song.

The mercurial Sandy as I remember
her when we were an item – seen
here about a year before I met her.

Underwear Parade. The boys
clowning around one night after
a few too many at the bar.

The Leonards around 1980, about a year after I left Kimberley – clockwise
from left: Anthony, Lyell junior, Lyell senior, Sandra and mom Phyllis.

Magirus with myself, Ian, James and Alan in view, performing in our band "stepouts", or formal band uniforms. The shirts were red and the pants black.

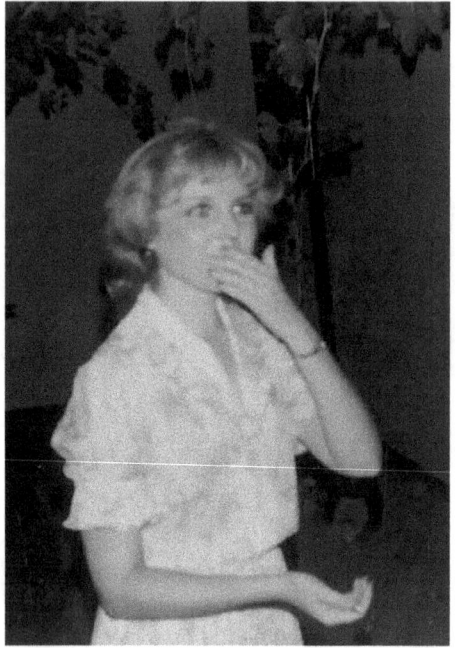

The beautiful Sandra "Sandy" Leonard – the inspiration for my song "November."

In the eyes of the beholder - the beautiful, charming and feisty Caroline, at around the time we were together.

The inimitable John Ferrier: friend and amiable rival in music. Seen here in action with Magirus playing Bass, with Ian in the background on his Telecaster.

John today.

The first barn dance we did for the Young Lions. Front row L-R: Willie Els, Nick Vlok, Dave, Vincent, Kevin Jarmin and Pete. Back Row L-R: James, Alan, Ian, Eddie and me, smiling sarcastically and looking a bit camp as a result, due to the fact that Sandy and I had just split up and I was in no mood for photos, or for that matter, to party. I had a cigarette in my right hand.

Three of the Olsweska siblings – Diane, Quenton and the sensuous Glynis, my delightful distraction after my break with Sandy – seen here a few years after I left Kimberley.

The Olsweskas. Clockwise seated L-R: Granddad Syd, the gorgeous Valerie, dad, granddad, mom and Quenton. Standing at the rear are Ida, the siblings step-grandmother, and the beautiful and demure Glynis.

Yours truly at one of the last barn dances we did for the Young Lions, around February 1979. L-R: Myself, Alan, Malcolm on bass, James, who was also the caller, and Themi.

The band assigned to do Captain Stevens album in Jo'burg, May 1979, one month before I finished my two years national service. Seated: Captain Charles Stevens. Standing L-R: Themi Venturas (bass), Mike Bayes (trumpet), Robert Bailey (trumpet), James Thomas (trumpet), Alan Rolstone (cornet), Aubrey Boltman (keyboards), Malcolm Du Plessis (piano and musical arrangements), Dale Collins (drums). Inset: Myself on guitar, shown here at EMI playing my favourite guitar at the time, my Ibanez twelve string

The Leonards 2015
Clockwise L-R: Lourinda, Lyell's wife; myself, Anthony, Lyell junior and matriarch
Phyllis, with pet accessories. Sandy was in Cape Town with her family during my visit.

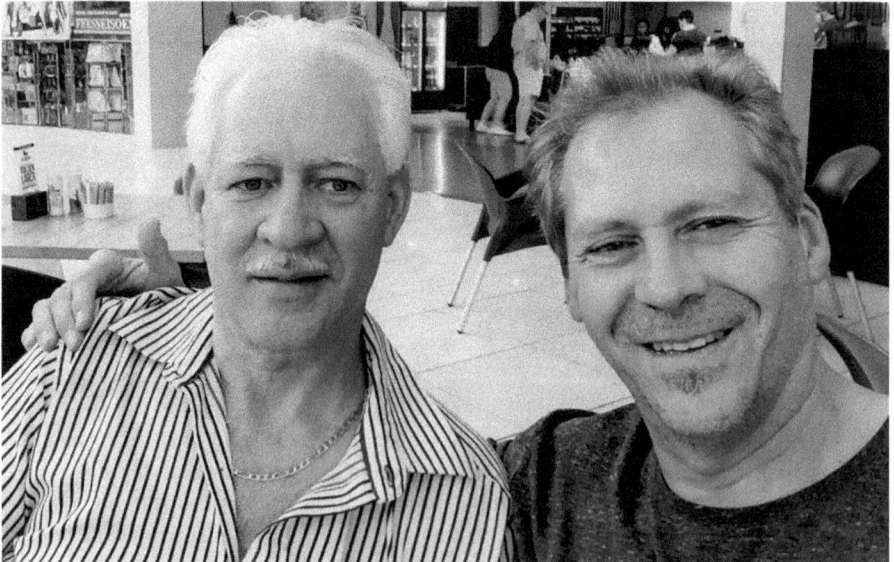

The two Magirus band leaders. Visiting Vincent in
Joburg on my trip to South Africa in 2015.

The National Service Officers and NCO's of 1 Maintenance unit –
otherwise known as Diskobolos - around April 1979. Yours truly top row,
eighth from the left. Hugh and Eddie are second row, first and second
from the right. Our Commandant is seated first row centre.

The Hotel Diskobolos.
Kimberley 2015.

The inside atrium at the Kimberley Sun (Garden Court).
Many Magirus gigs were performed at this venue.

Jack Hindon officers club, about 2 kilometres from the camp
- the scene of Magirus' last gig. Seen here in 2015.

Kimberley's main street in November 2015.
Right: The building (with glass bricks) that I had my drivers license issued in.
Back left: The old steel and glass Trust Bank building,
home of the Alarm Clock restaurant.

Our main hangout. The Kimberley Sun - now called Garden Court.
Kimberley 2015

The main gates of Diskobolos, a photo taken very discreetly after I was chased
away by the guards, citing security reasons. The guardhouse is on the right.
Kimberley 2015

I'M NOT SAYING GOODBYE

As the weeks wore on after the Kate Bush incident with Sandy, and the first week of October had rolled around, I was noticing that things were not all well in our love camp. One Sunday night at a cheese and wine party hosted by Brenda Applewhite (or Nipplepink, as Ian liked to call her) and the young Lions Club of Kimberley, I was particularly aware of her disquiet. The young Lions Club, by the way, was almost exclusively responsible for about 70% of our gigs—they absolutely loved us and showed it by hiring us for almost every function they put on, which was an average of twice monthly! As this night wore on, Sandy's distance and aloofness was interspersed with bouts of annoyance at me. She was constantly nagging me to give up smoking, and I would just dig my heals in. I did try my charm, answering her complaints with longsuffering understanding, all the while trying to figure out what the problem was.

Still, in my mind, the party was just another romantic interlude with this very enigmatic lady, and did not prepare me for the following weekend. The weekend came with me looking forward to a whole weekend of the Leonards' hospitality—my little refuge from reality—with Mrs.' wonderful meals, and very little in the way of interruptions for me and my little inamorata. Sailing through Friday night and then the whole of Saturday and Saturday night, which, I might add, was just blissful, nothing prepared me for Sunday morning's announcement:

"I think we need to stop seeing each other." "What??!! What's wrong??" I stammered." Nothing. I just don't think it's a good idea to continue," she replied."Why? I thought things were great between

91

us!" I said in an almost pleading voice. "I can't see you anymore," she said.

"Can you just tell me why? Did I do something wrong?" I was in panic mode!

"No," came the obscure reply.

"Then what is it?" I asked, confused and heartbroken.

"Nothing. We just need a break from each other!" she said again.

No reason was given, but I wasn't leaving until I got a one. It wasn't forthcoming, so I carried on with the guesses—most of the day! We had lunch. I entreated both Mrs. and Anthony, who was visiting. They just smiled wryly and said, "You know Sandra...stubborn!" I resumed my interrogation. No success, until I finally asked whether or not it was because of her Matric final exams. That seemed to spark some acknowledgement, but I wasn't sure whether or not this was the real reason she wanted to break up with me. I was devastated. Floored. But this was the excuse offered and because I was so blindly in love, I worked with that." So you'd rather have no distractions for your exams?" I asked, in a futile attempt to almost create an excuse for her behavior."Yes,"came the abrupt reply."Do we have to break up totally? Can we not get back together after we've had a break?""We'll see," she said."How about towards the end of November? You'll be finished your exams then!?" I was desperate..."I don't know Clive. Maybe..." "Alright," I said. "November, then... Can I have one last kiss before I leave?"

That kiss was so bittersweet, but at least she still wanted to kiss me goodbye. I left, feeling like my stomach had been sliced open. What was I going to do without my girl on weekends? What was I going to do without my Kimberley family? This was my fortress, my home away from home, my sanctuary from the camp! I suddenly realised that I'd hardly been to my real home in Joburg for some time. I was pretty consumed with life in Kimberley even though it was army life. It had been really good.

As far as the rest of my friends were concerned, they had been getting on with their lives while I had been ensconced with Sandy and her family. On Tuesday that next week, Alan, Pete, Dave and I went into town on army "business"—some routine run that should have taken us, at the most, two hours—but we managed to stretch it out to three. After our run, Pete made a turn towards the suburb of Cassandra (like I needed a reminder!!) and stopped at a house with a huge pavement service area at the front of it. The house was a single level three bedroom with a short staircase leading up from the path to the front door. The boys rang the bell and a stout, jolly black-haired lady with a huge smile answered the door.

"Hello boys! Glynis?! Your army friends are here!"

I wasn't quite prepared for my next emotion...

This swarthy girl with lustrous hair, built in all the right places, with a smile as big as her mother's, swung around the corner. And the voice, that voice—teasingly husky with a bubbly laugh from that inviting mouth, with mother-of-pearl perfect teeth.

"Hi!"

I was in lust! We went and sat in the lounge, and Pete and Alan launched into a patter of familiarity with her. A rather shy, pretty schoolgirl ambled awkwardly in and quietly sat at the adjoining dining room table and pulled some homework out of her school bag. This was Glynis' sister, Diane. Diane's shyness made her almost unnoticeable until one night in the Kimberley Hotel when she got into flirtatious mode—something I had not witnessed before—and proved herself as great a kisser as her sister! Not with me, mind, but with Alan, who I think she fancied quite a bit. She certainly treated us to a show, and succeeded in making us all jealous of Alan! I later discovered that Glynis had two other siblings, the eternally gorgeous and wise-beyond-her-years Valerie, and the youngest, a boy, Quenton. Their mother was on her own, as their parents, though still married, were living separate lives, their father living and working in Joburg. Our visits and excursions with Glynis and her friends in tow were, from that time forward, numerous and varied. But for now, I still needed to re-focus.

The weekend after Sandy's and my semi break-up, I decided to go home to visit the family and get around to see some of my friends. It was good to be home among the familiar and to catch up with everyone, especially my mom, who I think was wondering whether or not she was going to see me again. That Friday, I went with an old girlfriend of mine from school, Debbie, and her new beau, a good friend of mine by the name of Brett Schaeffer, out to movies with some mutual friends. She already knew of our band and asked me if we'd be interested in playing for my old high school's Matric Dance. She was on the committee to organise the entertainment, and if I knew Debbie, things would be handled professionally. I jumped at the chance. We discussed price, which would be a little more expensive, being Joburg, and I promised I would seek permission from the captain to do the function. She would discuss everything with the school. What a homecoming this would be if it worked out...

On Saturday morning my old school mate Ronny dropped in to see me. He was accompanied by a guy named Clifton, whom he knew from Pomona, a suburb of Kempton consisting mainly of small holdings. Ronny was heading into town and asked if I wanted to join them. Hanging around Kempton City doing nothing? OK, sounded like a plan. Clifton had a small brown Renault which we all piled into and headed off. Before we went into town, Clifton decided he needed to get something from home. A little way from his house he turned into a small holding with a long white split-paling fence. A long single story house was situated at the end of the short driveway. We all piled out and went up to the door and Clifton rang the doorbell. Floor time again... This gorgeous creature with curly blonde shoulder-length hair answered the door. Clifton chatted to her for a bit and then we left.

"Who was THAT?" I enquired. "THAT was Caroline!" Ronny replied. "But forget about her. You don't stand a chance!"

Clifton smiled in agreement. Now two things people should never say to me: "Impossible", and "You don't stand a chance!" Already my mind was turning over and my determination was surfacing. After watching Clifton buy three LP's at Look and Listen, followed by a lunch at the local Spur, we headed back to Clifton's place. His dad was a drummer, so we sat around chatting to him and listening to Clifton's new records. Somehow, we wound up going back to

Caroline's place, which, as I mentioned, was just down the road. This time we went inside and spent a little more time there talking to Caroline and her younger sister Aimlee.

Things were winding up and I wasn't sure whether there was any interest there. We'd said a few words about my stint in the army and exchanged a few smiles, but that was all. Clifton was getting into the car and Ronny was heading for the passenger door. I had to act! It was now or never! I didn't know when I'd be home again, and whether or not someone else would steal a march on me with this beauty.

Summoning all my courage, I yelled to Ronny "Hold on..." I turned to her and said: "Listen, could I get your phone number?" She looked at me with a twinkle in her magnificent blue eyes.

"Sure". She went to a table, grabbed a paper and pen, and scribbled down her phone number and handed it to me with a grin. I was over the moon. Ronny was extremely unimpressed and muttered all the way back to my place. Clifton just drove. I think I'd made my point.

NOVEMBER'S COMING ROUND

When I got back to camp, the first thing I did was gather our band members together and let them know of the possibility of playing in Joburg for my old school. Everyone's ears picked up. Vincent got particularly excited and we chatted wildly about the event and its details. We discussed how we were going to broach the subject with the captain. We had no idea what he would say. Being a realist, I decided that even though it was my gig I would let Vincent do the talking because if anyone stood any chance of selling the idea to the Cap it would be him. As I mentioned earlier, the captain was in awe of Vince, so we stood a good chance.

Later that week we knocked on his door and presented the offer. We did talk it up somewhat, saying how prestigious this would be for the camp, etc. He looked at us with a piercing stare and finally agreed, on condition that we were accompanied by a PF officer. We agreed, but reluctantly, until we found out that it would be the amiable Lieutenant Breedt—which didn't make it so much an issue anymore. I contacted Debbie and told her that we had the all clear. In turn, she told me that the school had also given her the OK. The dance would be on the Friday of the second weekend of November. Vincent then had the brainwave of contacting his agent in Joburg to organise a gig for the Saturday night of that same weekend there. What he didn't tell me was that he was not going to inform the captain of this! Consequently, when we had our last meeting with the captain to finalise the transport and accommodation arrangements, I started asking questions about the meal arrangements at Vincent's gig, and got kicked under the table by both Vincent, and then Ian, who I'm sure had no idea why Vincent was doing it in the first place—

if Vincent was doing it, then it must be right! The Cap gave me a quizzical look and then the meeting continued. I was highly annoyed and afterwards took them to task about it. Vincent explained (finally) that we were doing this gig "under the table", with no money going to the camp—only to us. I suppose that was worth a bit of pain.

The one fly in the ointment was that we couldn't take all the guys with us. Aside from Vincent and me, we had to choose which of the band was going with us, as we couldn't take everyone. Pete, Alan, James, Eddie, Dave, Nick, Ian and Huey were the guys that made the cut. Amongst others, a very annoyed JB Ferrier wasn't included, as wasn't Malcolm, who didn't seem to mind too much. We were set! Ian and Huey celebrated by pissing on each other in the shower that night, and Ferrier chose to annoy me with rancid remarks, much to his amusement, until I told him I was glad he wasn't coming with!

"Fuck you, Clive Hay! You KNOW that's the one thing I wanted to do!"

You wouldn't believe that we're best friends still to this day!

In the meantime, my romantic life was becoming slightly complicated. Things were always feast or famine with me. I'd started phoning Caroline on a regular basis, and having incredible conversations with her for over an hour. I would often phone reverse the charges, and to this day I don't know what her father thought of the phone bill. In Kimberley, my visits to Glynis and her family became more numerous and intense, with her consoling me over my broken-hearted wonderings about why Sandy and I weren't an item anymore. She developed an interest in me mainly, I think, because I was still hankering after Sandy, and I was a prize to be won, and then, I suspect, discarded after I had turned my attentions fully to her. She was a notorious tease and a flirt, which both angered and enticed me, but I managed to keep cool for most of the time, except when she kissed me and nearly sucked my tongue out of my head! My imagination went wild, and I have to admit that my interest in Glynis was mostly sexual. Mostly? Well, almost entirely! But I did like her and loved her family for the same reason I loved Sandy's—we were always welcome, and made to feel like this was our home away from home. On the other hand, Caroline didn't really know about Sandy, and at that stage, I don't think she would've really cared much, so I didn't bore her with the details, or run the risk of losing my options with her at that point in time... The politics of love!

In the meantime, however, my heart was really still in Sandy's possession, and I would still phone her and ask if I could come over. The receptions to my calls were either cool or warm. I could never tell what was awaiting me on the other side of the phone line, but I grasped at any little chance I got. Finally one night I asked her if I could see her one Wednesday night. She agreed, and Dave Oldham and I went over. She was the ice-princess! I felt like I was a total stranger being held at bay, and that, in fact, she was a little irritated by my presence. Finally, I asked if I could come over that Friday night, which was greeted with a totally indifferent "If you like!"

I looked at her like a wounded hound, and said, "OK, bye..."

She hardly even look at me when she farewelled me. I got into the car a defeated, angry nineteen year-old. I said to Dave, "Well, looks like this is it. She's not interested." Dave gave me a reassuring pat on the shoulder and we drove back to camp in silence.

I decided, in light of my Wednesday night experience, not to go to Sandy's place that Friday night; maybe I should just wait a bit and see how I felt going forward. My thinking was, even if I was expected I wouldn't be greeted enthusiastically, and quite frankly, I thought a big "Up Yours!" was the appropriate action to take, and that I wouldn't be missed. Anyway, I had a sexually charged, if tenuous, relationship with Glynis, and I had an ever-growing liking for this beauty from Pomona, whose father would, I was sure, send me a huge phone bill one day!

That same Sunday night a bunch of us wound up at the De Lange's house. Karen's dad owned the Alarm Clock restaurant in the Trust Bank building in the centre of town, and because of our association with the family (and Vincent's burgeoning affair with Karen), we would often go and eat there, or just visit their house. I have to say that I was not as regular a visitor as Vincent and the others, being ensconced in my own social serendipities, but Mr. De Lange would use our services from time to time. I have to say that he was also one of the reasons I didn't pursue much contact with them, being a somewhat loud and overbearing character. We didn't click. That night, however, I wound up having a few drinks at their house, and my slightly inebriated thoughts strayed towards my Sandy. The best part of our relationship (and the beer) got the better of me and I asked if I could use the phone. Permission granted, I got a querying look from Vincent, who, I have to say, had my best interests at heart. Everyone knew of our break up, and now the chorus grew:

"Don't do it Clive!"

I did it anyway. The phone rang and Mademoiselle picked it up. "Hi!" I said in a lovelorn voice.

"Don't you 'Hi' me, Clive Hay."

"What's wrong?" I asked quizzically.

"Where were you on Friday night??" came the charged question...

"I didn't seem very welcome, so I decided to go to movies with Alan and Pete!" I said emphatically.

"We were expecting you to—"

I cut her off :" Well I'll come over when I'm more welcome. You didn't exactly want to see me on Friday anyway, judging by your comments and behaviour on Wednesday night!!"

"Excuse me!!" she sharply retorted." My mom made supper for you and prepared a room for you and the whole family was waiting to see you!!"

I stopped short..."Alright then, please apologise to your mom for me. I'll see you sometime next week, maybe..."

" Clive, if you're not at my house in the next half an hour, then don't bother coming here again!!" Click. She hung up.

"Don't go, don't go!!" came a choir of voices behind me. I turned around. All I saw was a sea of faces. Everyone had been listening to my conversation!

"Aaaagh, I'd better go." I said reluctantly.

"Clive you're crazy! I'm warning you, it's the wrong thing to do!" said Ian in a concerned manner.

I headed for the door.

"Alright, but you'll be sorry!" came the reply from Hugh.

I asked Dave if he would give me a lift, then decided I wasn't going to be there in thirty minutes. She could wait an hour.

After cursing, complaining and hanging around for a while, I signalled Dave to take me there. We got there in about fifteen minutes—approximately half an hour after the deadline. The picture that greeted me has stayed with me to this day: Sandra answered the door with the biggest grin I'd seen on her face for a long time. She was clearly pleased to see me, and had obviously been expecting me. I say obviously because she looked ravishing, although her relief was also palpable! She was wearing the same outfit that she'd had on the first time I went to visit her at home—a white short-sleeved off the shoulder top with blue jeans and heeled sandals. She very tenderly kissed me hello and grabbed my hand, still grinning with relief that I had come.

I was like putty in hers, but could still summon a bit of resolve to act annoyed: "Oh, so NOW you're happy to see me!! Don't turn on the charm. I thought you were supposed to be mad with me!!"

"Well..." she answered with some resolve, but just enough to not make me get defensive, "my mom was upset too..."

"Yes, I know. Sorry Phyllis," I said to her mom who was also standing there smiling.

"That's OK Clive," said her ever gracious mother.

It was an interesting evening for me, because in my mind this was the smoothing out of the break-up. We were friends again, and there was still some good familiarity between us without it being overly romantic. I didn't know it then, but she did not share my outlook.

After that night, I was comfortable with seeing less of Sandy and playing the field a bit, with Glynis in particular. Things were definitely hotting up on that side, but we were both also keeping our options open. I was OK with that because of my phone calls to Pomona. Still, Glynis was immediately accessible, and I was going to her house with Dave, Alan and Pete more regularly now.

One fateful Sunday Glynis asked me to go with her to the Aquatic Club at Riverton, just outside Kimberley. I'd never been there, but had heard quite a bit about it from the Leonards, who frequented it quite often. I only found out it was called the AQUATIC Club when I saw the sign on arrival. Mrs. Leonard always referred to it as the "KWADDY Club", which always had an air of mystery about it. On this day, however, the sun was out and the whole area was green from the spring thunderstorms. Glynis was flirting big time with me, walking hand in hand, arm in arm, and stopping every so often to suck my tongue right out of my head! At some stage after her inquiry, when I was telling her about my status quo with Sandy, she ducked her head and pulled me along suddenly, half laughing and saying embarrassedly, "Oh my God, there she is, there she is!! Come on, let's go!!"

I was somewhat slow to respond, because I didn't know what she was talking about at first. "What are you doing?" I asked. Then in horror, it dawned on me. I turned around to see Sandy, head down, running in the opposite direction. She was obviously visiting with her family. I felt awful. But I felt a strange mixture of wonder and guilt when I looked up at Glynis and realised: Glynis had long black hair! Sandy's earlier dream had not been about Kate Bush, but about Glynis!

What does one make of these things? I don't know, but I felt a strange sense of empowerment over the emotional chains that still bound me to my mystery girl. I don't know if it was because she had seen me with Glynis, or whether she genuinely cared, but she later told me that that was the time period that she was most in love with me. She was and is to this day an enigma, which is such a draw card for me, and I think, for most men. I was lucky enough to have shared a few special months with this incredible girl, and the mystery of her and the memory of her will last a lifetime.

WHEN WE SAW WHAT
WAS MEANT TO BE

A ctually, the Cap and the band had been getting along pretty well at this point of our time together. So well, in fact, that he invited us to a party at his house. To put this into perspective, it was tantamount to being invited to the Prime Minister's house. PF officers throwing a party for enlisted men? Come on! But there we were, a bunch of young, cocky rascals being feted by the army's elite! OK then! Time to get organised. The powers that be quite obviously knew of our shenanigans, and so the captain announced that we could bring our girlfriends. Hmm... Problem was, I didn't have one. Glynis was the closest I had to a girlfriend then, but we were both in the twilight zone of commitment. I did invite her though, and it was almost taken for granted (by me, anyway) that she was my date. She took the invitation a bit more generally. When the invitation was issued, Dave Oldham and I were sitting around at her moms place. Now Glynis had one hell of a beautiful school friend, Deolinda Fourie, who happened to be visiting her the day we were there. We'd met her a few weeks earlier, and, to be honest, with her and Glynis around, I felt like a bit of a kid in a candy store, not knowing who to choose. Because of how far I'd come with Glynis however, I didn't think it polite to show too much interest in Deolinda, so instead, I brought in Dave Oldham to help out. I sat both Glynis and Deolinda down and told them about the party at the captain's house and that they were both coming! I then proceeded to then tell Dave that he was taking Deolinda, and Deolinda that she was going with Dave! The consternation on both of their faces was hilarious, and was followed by somewhat muted protest from both of them:

"But Clive, I'm sure Deolinda might not want to go with me...!"

"Yes, But what if Dave doesn't want to go with me...!"

"No buts! All settled. You two are going with each other!" I said firmly.

Dave: "Are you ok with that Deolinda?"

Deolinda: "Ya, sure. If YOU'RE ok with that?!"

Dave: "Ya."

Me: "All right, settled then. It'll be fun."

Glynis was particularly pleased that her friend was coming. Methinks Dave was too! Chalk another one up for the Matchmaker.

That weekend, we had a gig in Upington, a large regional centre on the mighty Orange River. I wasn't prepared for the Orange. Our accommodation was in a caravan park right on the river. The reason I wasn't prepared for it is that Upington is in the middle of a semi-desert, and the place is like an oasis. This was late October as well—beginning of the rainy season—and so the town was looking clean, pretty and inhabited by greenery. But the river was spectacular. This huge body of water in the middle of the desert, and flowing right through the caravan park!

The gig covered both Friday and Saturday nights at the local army camp, and, as usual, we made a huge impression. After the Friday night gig we perused the town that Saturday morning for a music store in order to buy some guitar strings, had a burger for lunch at the local Wimpy, and then headed back to the caravan park. That afternoon has stayed in my memory all these years for two reasons: firstly, it was a beautiful day, and the river was sparkling alongside us as we all sat and chatted. The contrast of being in a semi-desert town with a majestic river fringed with impressive greenery was like witnessing something out of an Arabian Nights story. Secondly, a little later, I sauntered over to the pay phone and decided to make a collect call to Caroline. Talk about a serendipitous moment! We spoke like we were old friends, nay—more than friends—that wonderful moment in a burgeoning relationship where you know you've made an impression, and that special other person has left an impression! That feeling where you know that something good is busy happening, and that all is right in your world. I left that conversation more convinced than ever that I was onto a sure thing. This was an impressive girl in more ways than one! Joburg was looming, and during that phone call I learned that Caroline was going to be at the Matric farewell... The night of the captain's party arrived. It was decided to hold it on the Tuesday night, as we were headed for Joburg that Friday. We all spruced ourselves up in our civvies and then headed off to get our girls. I'm still amazed to this day that the army and military police were so slack that they didn't pick up the fact that we were enlisted men, basically impersonating officers! No one seemed to care. It didn't matter. We were so used to the status quo that it would have been a major shock if we had been arrested.

To be honest, I wasn't sure that my matchmaker instincts regarding Dave and Deolinda had been correct. After all, I was really role-playing when I hooked them up together, secretly wishing it was me who was with her. She was a real beauty and she and Dave seemed oddly mismatched, she being quite tall and striking, and Dave being on the short side, somewhat melancholy, and with a mouthful of false teeth, no less. (He'd had a serious gum disease and needed to have them removed when he was sixteen). Don't get me wrong, Oldham wasn't ugly by any stretch of the imagination, but there was another difference—he was from a strong English-speaking Eastern Cape 1820 settler background, and she from an Afrikaans family. It couldn't work, could it? How wrong I was, as it turned out!

After picking the girls up we headed back towards the camp. The captain's house was six kilometres past the camp at another military installation called the Danie Theron combat school. We arrived at a fairly plain red brick house, so typical of the PF accommodation. The captain greeted us at the door with his wife, a very gracious and hospitable blonde lady by the name of Sonia, who showed us into the lounge, where a small smorgasbord had been laid out. Everyone piled into the booze first of course, and pretty soon the party was well under way. Vincent had brought Diane with him, and the other guys had some dates with them who I hadn't met before. We carried on partying, dancing and chatting for a couple of hours, until I noticed that Glynis was getting slightly loose in her behaviour—a result, no doubt, of a bit too much wine! As a matter of fact, she was all over my best mate Alan, which pissed me off no end, and embarrassed Alan. Even though we weren't exactly a tight item, I did consider her my date, as did Alan, and I proceeded to tell her that if she persisted in carrying on like this, she wasn't going to see me again. This produced a drunken cry of remorse accompanied by much clinging and begging for a second chance. I knew that this behaviour was just part of Glynis's drink-addled state and that the flirtation with Alan was part of that, but I decided to play the hard-ass a bit anyway.

"No, no, don't flirt with Alan then come crying to me!" I said as I turned away, with her desperately grabbing at me and crying somewhat hysterically. What I found somewhat amusing was Dave and Deolinda's slightly awkward and embarrassed attempts to quiet Glynis's drunken ravings, and their efforts to get her into the car and take her home, at which they eventually succeeded, with much muttering about her current demeanor. Their first project as a couple! I accompanied them, mainly due to the fact that I was somewhat embarrassed as well and felt responsible for her current state—she WAS with me after all, and all this in front of my CO!

I wasn't really that annoyed with Glynis. She was a vibrant, sexy and interesting girl, and our friendship has lasted to this day, along with her wonderful family. In retrospect, I suppose I wanted to have my cake and eat it. I was at a metaphoric crossroads with three girls standing at each junction, and I had to make a choice. Perhaps the choice was in my own imagination, and they didn't feel the same way about me that I felt about them, but I was pretty confident that I had some bankability with all three ladies—Sandy, Glynis and Caroline—and that I was in a position to choose which road to travel. Even though Sandy and I had broken up, my encounter with her at the Aquatic Club convinced me that there were still feelings there. I wasn't sure yet just which road to take—the blonde mystery, the dark-haired siren, or the quiet, but impressive girl-next-door... My trip to Joburg was about to make my mind up for me.

THE EYES OF THE BEHOLDER

———————— ▸◂ ————————

That Friday morning we all piled into our transports and headed for the Big Smoke. Joburg is a city built on a pile of gold and situated on a plateau 1753 metres above sea level. It was the love of my life, as far as cities in South Africa were concerned. Being from Durban originally, the discovery of Joburg as a young boy when my family moved there filled me with awe and wonder. This was a city! I loved the Highveld—the name of its general geographical location—I loved its cosmopolitan blend of peoples, I loved what it had to offer anyone fortunate enough to live there. It was the biggest and the best in the whole of Africa! The rest of South Africa's big cities were provincial by comparison. Joburg was the centre of my universe. At the time, I lived on the East Rand in one of the towns that ran close to the mining vein, but not on it. Kempton Park was home to South Africa's only international airport at that time, so it was a vibrant, prosperous township.

We rolled into town that afternoon and headed straight for the function hall in Bonaero Park, a suburb of Kempton, and proceeded to unload and set up. As we walked in, Debbie, who was obviously pleased to see us, came up to greet us with a huge grin. I kissed her hello and introduced her to everyone. She was such a great girl, and quite obviously had very good organisational skills. The hall was immaculately decked out in an aviation theme—very fitting for the location. After chatting to her for a bit, finalising details and scouting the stage, we set up and did a thorough sound check—something I insisted on, as my reputation was at stake.

Having finished, we all went our separate ways to get ready for the evening. I'd organised for Alan and Pete to stay at my folks place with me. So, followed by Lieutenant Breedt in his car, which he had driven down himself, we headed off to Allen Grove where my mom and stepfather were waiting for us. After introductions, I showed Alan and Pete their sleeping arrangements—one in my brother's room and the other on the couch—and we all had an early dinner together. Lieutenant Breedt had his own sleeping arrangements, which suited me somewhat, as I wasn't really relishing the thought of sharing digs with the authority! My parents, I have to say, found the lieutenant very amusing, but were friendly and accommodating. I've never seen him so nervous! He kept on about his shoes and how they didn't fit him too well, and stuttered through a lot of the conversation.

After dinner, we got into our band uniforms—red formal shirt, black trousers and black shoes—jumped into the car and headed off to the hall again. When we got there we were greeted by the glorious sight of young adults getting ready to take their place in the world which, tonight, was definitely their oyster. The rest of the band joined us and ran around excitedly, making sure the gear was all set up properly, while hoping to make an impression on the beautiful girls that adorned the hall. Debbie came to greet me and re-introduce me to my old Headmaster, Mr. Roehrs—it was only two short years since he had pulled Debbie and me into his office in a rage and berated us because we had been caught snogging in assembly. After dispensing with the pleasantries, I was happy to get back to the stage to get the night underway.

Besides, there was only one person I really wanted to see—and there she was! Sitting at the second table on the right hand side of the stage—Caroline! She smiled at me in such a way that it was almost like there was just her and me, and no one else in that room... Ah the love of youth, the excitement of young romance! To be honest, I can't even remember if she had a date that night, or if I was her date. She looked stunning. A mass of blonde curls in a floral knee length dress with white heels. I climbed the steps to the stage and we proceeded with dinner music. To keep things smooth we did a lot of muzak-styled songs with me on acoustic twelve-string, which brought disdainful, dismissive looks from some of the guys there. One guy in particular who was sitting near the stage had one of those "so impress me, 'cos you haven't so far" looks on his face. I remember playing "Just the Way You Are" and almost getting scowled at. Not that it bothered me—Caroline was sending very approving glances my way! First break came and I made a beeline for her table. After weeks of talking to each other on the phone, would the magic work face to face? You betcha!

In many ways, I was in my comfort zone. I had my band mates with me, playing at my old school with so many people I knew and loved, and here I was with this beauty - another enigma to unwrap! At that stage in my life, women had a hard time figuring me out. I wasn't your average male in my approach to women. Indeed, I was very quietly confident and calculating in my approach, and almost always succeeded in charming my way into their curves by really just being myself. Oh the testosterone was there, but I wasn't letting on for a minute! It was a veil that I patiently wore until my subject was warmed up. A typical line that came my way on many occasions was, "You're different—I've never met a guy like you before..." The rest of the sentence was often muted by the presence of my tongue in her mouth. Of course, it never went to my head... Yeah, right! But honestly, I was confident enough to take rejection if it was offered, and nice enough to take acceptance if that was on offer.

However, some of God's unbelievably exotic feminine handiwork often throw you left-arm spinners, and this was one of them. I knew she was interested, but I wasn't sure how much, so I kept it friendly but calm. We both knew the dance steps to this one, but it was just a question as to who was leading whom. Conversation was lively and mysterious at the same time. Who was this girl? She was definitely becoming more interesting to me by the minute!

After returning to the stage, I picked up my electric guitar and we opened with "Fantasy", by Earth, Wind and Fire. The atmosphere changed immediately, and everyone was on the dance floor. I even got knowing and approving looks from the guy near the stage who had been dissing us earlier. We had everyone in the palm of our hands and we were cruising. The only fly in the ointment was in between one of our songs, when two pissheads facing each other at Caroline's table started having a kicking contest under the table, which quickly turned into seated fisticuffs, with little regard for my beloved who was sitting close by and very nearly in the line of fire. The whole thing didn't last too long, but it was typical of some of the Kempton locals to prove to those in their immediate vicinity that they didn't have the intellect to sort out their problems like smart people.

As for the rest of the evening, it was nothing but a triumph. I was the local lad who they all knew had one musical talent, who had gone off to the army and returned to them with ten musical talents! But who am I to take credit? We had two fine drummers, a great brass section, excellent keysmen and competent guitarists, and when we played to a willing audience we more than rose to the occasion. And Debbie? We made her look like a genius for hiring us, and the compliments flew.

After packing up, Alan and Pete followed Caroline and me back to her place to see her home. (Turns out I was her date!) Caroline had a brand new Mazda 323 (a gift from father, which I shall cover in a bit more detail soon), and I had the privilege of driving it that night. I didn't yet have my driver's license, but was in the process of learning, and little did I know that this was the car I was going to get the most practice in... We got to her place and parked. I then proceeded to invite her to lunch the next day, and then to our gig on the Saturday night. I'll never forget her answer. "I'd love to. What time?"

I said 10am for the lunch part, and 7pm for the gig.

"OK. If you're late, though, don't bother coming to pick me up. I don't abide tardiness!"

Wow! We got out of the car and I walked her to her front door. I restrained myself from the goodnight kiss. I still wasn't 100% sure of my standing in this regard and I didn't want to spoil my chances. It was a warm farewell though, and I looked forward to the next day. I hopped into Pete's car and we went home.

Next morning we woke to the typical sumptuous breakfast that my wonderful mom prepared for us. My mother. What a wise and loving person she was and still is, greatly respected by her friends and colleagues. I didn't know it then, but these were going to be our last precious months together as a family before she and my stepfather moved out of my life as a nurturing influence who provided a shelter for me outside the army. We had a small, but accommodating three bedroom house in Allen Grove, a quiet, middle class suburb in Kempton, which seemed to be the local magnet for my friends once I moved out of boarding school and attended our local high school. At this stage, this was still the status quo in my life—people coming and going.

This morning, however, I was renewed with fresh vigour. After breakfast, we all piled into the car and headed off to Caroline's house to pick her up, after which the four of us headed for the city. When we got there, about forty minutes after leaving, we drove up Commissioner Street and parked at the Carlton Centre, at that time the tallest building in Africa—all of fifty stories high. Inside the Carlton was one of the biggest music stores in the city, Bothners. We went inside and played around with some of the instruments, bought some guitar strings, and then went to get some lunch. Conversation was dry, witty, amusing and full of the joys of three late teen guys and one beautiful girl in her final school year sharing each other's good company.

I was smitten. I'm pretty sure Pete and Alan were as well, but were always respectfully friendly. Alan Rolstone. Probably my best friend in the world, then and now. Quiet, intelligent, calm. I was always a little in awe of the calmness, in particular. There should be more like him in the world, but aren't. Pete Auths. Possibly one of the nicest human beings anyone could meet. Always accommodating and friendly to a fault. Pete was always nice to me, even when I wasn't particularly kind to him. Also—still friends today.

Part of our plan on our way back home was to stop at Alan's sister's flat in Berea, next to Hillbrow—Joburg's nightlife hotspot—and I was feeling very much like I wanted to kiss this girl sitting next to me but had to wait for the opportune moment. Holding hands was not an issue at this stage but I was getting anxious to assess the situation properly. We arrived at Alan's sister's place and proceeded in the lift to the sixth floor, where her and her husband's apartment was. After being greeted at the door and ushered in, we all stood around and chatted for a bit, after which Caroline and I retired to the balcony to check out the view. After surveying the surrounds, but more importantly, the scenery in my immediate vicinity, I suddenly made my move—only to be rebuffed by a head of blonde curls shyly turned away. I blew it! "You idiot!", I said to myself, and then soberly and embarrassedly turned away. Caroline excused herself and went off to the bathroom, while I stood foolishly outside on the balcony for a few more minutes. Somehow, I didn't feel like the deal had been blown completely, yet I resigned myself to the strong possibility that maybe this girl wasn't as interested in me as I was in her. Why was she spending this time with us, though? Was this just a test to see if I was worth further investigation—that I had just flunked? Ah well, I was still with my friends, which was some consolation. At which point in these thoughts of mine, Alan decided to sneak behind me and give me a wet willy—where you wet your finger and stick it in someone's ear—one of his and Pete's favourite tricks. Only this time, the finger was decidedly wetter and thicker - in fact, it was a tongue! I turned to protest—this was taking things too far! I looked for him, as only Caroline, who had reappeared, was standing outside with me. He must have ducked back in very quickly! I looked at the door, only to see Al some distance away in the lounge sitting on the sofa, deep in conversation with his sister and her husband. I suddenly noticed that Caroline was standing very close to me with a huge grin on her face—and it dawned on me...

When the smooching started after that, Caroline and I hardly came up for air until she was dropped off at home. We still had tonight's gig to get through, and, judging by this breakthrough, I had evidently passed the test, whatever it was. Wow!

The drive to the gig that night was in Pete's car, with four band members and my now official girlfriend. I must be honest, I didn't really see where we were going—too busy in the back seat! Amidst the witty conversation, Pete managed to hurt himself or spill something on himself, and he let out a choice expletive, which received a sharp rebuke from me—never in the presence of a lady! He apologised, but it was all very light-hearted, and we all laughed. It was one of those perfect nights. Everyone in the band was trying to show off in front of Caroline, which made me smile. I remember Vincent's comment from the previous night, about how impressed he was with the girls at my old school, and obviously Caroline was no exception. He did a great job that night of taking the lead to entertain the party we were playing at, by getting the people there to participate in some inane, but highly amusing games. I was impressed! He really had a way with an audience. One of my most enduring memories that night was during one of our breaks. Caroline and I were sitting on a stairway at the back of the hall, having a warm conversation. I really couldn't figure out what this beauty saw in a national service lance-corporal who played in a band.

"Two things—I don't know what to make of you—you're different." Ah! I was a mystery to her—not a typical guy. "And you're very ambitious—I like that!" Ambitious? I didn't know that I was, but I took that as a compliment from a very impressive girl. Late teens and early twenties are a wonderful time in young people's lives. I and many others like me were on the threshold of the promises that only youth can hold out to us, and it was a world full of possibilities and promises, with nothing to hold us back!

That night, on the way back from the gig, I wondered if I would be permitted to explore this burgeoning relationship a little further, so tentatively, in the middle of a passionate kiss, I slipped a hand under Caroline's blouse. No resistance. I suddenly realised she wasn't wearing a bra, and my hand came into contact with one of the most magnificent breasts known to man! Well, certainly to this man... Surely, another barrier had been tested and crossed, and the realisation dawned on me that this girl was as impressed with me as I was with her.

WHY DIDN'T WE TRY?

So began another romantic chapter in my life. For the first time in a long time, I was spending more weekends at home than in Kimberley—something I'm sure my mother was enjoying, as was I. And another event was unfolding—I was learning to drive. Back in camp, my experiences with this process were getting quite frustrating. My band mates who had cars were, I guess understandably, reluctant to let me use them on a regular basis. But more frustrating was that not one of them was a patient teacher, and so my time in cars chalking up experience was very limited, which didn't bode well for my chances of getting my learner's or driver's licenses. That is, until I met Caroline. Her dad was a sort of Jock Ewing, patriarchally overseeing his family of four girls like a hawk, checking out prospective suitors with intent, and dispensing with them by means of sarcasm and unsavoury nicknames if, in his mind anyway, they posed any kind of a threat—i.e. if his daughters were keen on them! He ran a construction company called Exclusive Erection—a name that caused my little miss no end of embarrassment ! But he was a successful businessman, and all the trappings of life available at the time were lavished on his girls, and his third-born was no exception. For passing her Matric exams and getting into College, Caroline was presented with the Mazda 323 I'd mentioned earlier—no small gift at the time, in view of the fact that there was a fuel crisis happening in the world. The Mazda 323, so the TV advertisements told us, could get to Cape Town—1500 km away, on one tank of fuel. This was a small, reliable, economical car—released onto the South African market only at the start of that year. This, methought, was one spoilt princess to be getting a gift such as this, and I was beginning to wonder whether I was viewed as a worthy suitor after all. Caroline's sisters also didn't settle for much less, so what she saw in me, I didn't know—but could I live up to it? Ah, the sisters. I only met the eldest one once, so I couldn't form an opinion. She seemed nice enough. The youngest, Aimlee, was the one who seemed most protective of Caroline and who was the most forthright in her opinions. And then there was Denise... I quite liked Denise. Caroline did not. Admittedly, when I was first warned about her, I was wary. The description I was given was that she was a cross between Joan Collins and Lucretia Borgia. Needless to say, when Caroline told me we had been invited to dinner at Denise's flat at the newly-built Ponte Towers, I was nervous. I wasn't even sure that Caroline wanted to go, but if this girl was ever mindful of anyone, it was her elder sister, and it seemed that Denise wanted to meet the new boyfriend! To make matters more nerve-wracking for me, I was going to be put on display in front of Denise's boyfriend, who would be, judging from her taste, a wealthy and successful individual. As we trepidaciously set off that night, I received further counselling on what to be aware of in the presence of Cruella De Ville. On arrival at Ponte's lifts, sensing my nervousness, Caroline hooked her arm through mine, grabbed my hand and drew me close with a big smile. I was still worried.

I needn't have been. Denise was a gracious hostess who made me feel at ease, and her paramour was convivial and engaging. Another reason for my apprehension was that I was a somewhat fussy eater, and was hoping against hope that whatever was put in front of me met with my limited culinary experience. Fortunately, dinner was delicious, and amidst much wine a jolly time was had by all. The only fly in the soufflé was the increasingly patronising verbal jabs that were pointed at Caroline by her sister. Tentatively, I came to the rescue as diplomatically, but as firmly as possible, letting Denise know in no uncertain terms that she must have been talking about someone else... The Caroline I knew was beautiful, witty and charming, as well as being extremely intelligent! Denise gave me a look of resigned disapproval, but was soon back to her own charming self.

To say I'd gained points that night is like saying that the Beatles were a popular band. The mixture of wine and hormones, not to mention that I'd stuck up for her at the risk of being excommunicated (or worse), made the drive home very amorous indeed! This girl was hooked! Actually, so was I. What was the next step? Well, for both of us, it wasn't as obvious as those of you reading this might think! Besides the sexual intent, I must take you back to Caroline's car. This part of the story became almost a part of the dance. By the time of our dinner with Denise, I was already driving the Mazda as a matter of course. In fact, madam was teaching me to drive while giving me free rein behind the wheel of her brand new car! Nearly every time we saw each other, I was in the driver's seat.

The instructions were hilarious, filled with sexual innuendo: "Try and get the rhythm between the clutch and the accelerator more relaxed. You've got to give me a smoooooth ride!"

Me: "Oh, I'll give you a smooth ride alright!"

Etc. We both laughed, but neither one of us was saying no. So there I was, in a sense taking advantage of the situation. Having said that, Caroline didn't seem to mind. Maybe she realised that she was the only one I knew giving me a chance to practice my driving skills on a regular basis. For heaven's sake, not even my own mother and stepfather were happy to let me use their car when I was at home! And by that time, I already had my learners license, which I had got just after the trauma of my breakup with Sandy. To this day, I don't know how I got it, because she had broken up with me two weeks before I was due to write it, and in my lovesick state I had given up all hope of concentrating on what I was supposed to learn.

In fact, the day I wrote my learner's I'd lost all pretense of having retained any information about the required driving and road instruction, so when I went to do it, I'd resigned myself to failure. Having been instructed by friends with licenses about how tough these one-on-one tests can be, and expecting to be seated in front of an instructor to verbally recite the rules of the road, imagine my intrigue and surprise when I was ushered into a room with about fifteen other nervous hopefuls! Turns out, one-on-ones weren't the fashion anymore. A paper was laid before us with multiple choice questions on the rules of the road and driving. I was still worried, and a little confused... Was this all we had to do, or was this a small lead-up to an even tougher one-on-one test once we'd finished the multiple choice? My worry started dissipating as soon as we were given the go-ahead to start answering the questions... The correct answers were pretty much plain common sense! Could it really be this easy? I finished before the end of the allotted time, feeling very chuffed that I'd completed what seemed to me to be a very easy exercise. My worries came back to haunt me though, when our instructor told us to lay down our pens and bring our papers to the front, where he proceeded to mark them. After what seemed like an hour, but was probably only fifteen minutes, he looked up, and what he said next made my heart sink:

"When I call your name, please stand up..."

He reached the end of a list of names, and mine wasn't among them! I sat there with the obvious notion that people who were asked to stand in these situations were about to be honoured with congratulations, and I was looking at having to repeat the process all over again. So much for my common sense! How wrong I was...

Instructor: "Those of you whose names I've called will have to repeat the test—the rest of you who are seated, congratulations—you've passed!

So, at least, Caroline had sitting in the driver's seat of her car someone who the Kimberley municipality had entrusted with learning the practicalities involved with driving an automobile.

Another happening that cemented, in my mind at least, that this was a girl who was more than a passing interest, was a conversation we were having one day. I'd just lit a cigarette and while we were talking, she stopped and said quietly: "You know, you shouldn't smoke if you're a singer. You could damage your voice." I stopped a while to absorb this. There was no irritation or sense of nagging in the statement. Just a quiet, passing concern that seemed to say "If you want to smoke, whom am I to stop you? I'm still here to support you, but this is not about me, it's about your future career." I don't know why, but I wanted to be strong for this girl. Show her that I could be decisive and single-minded about issues. In a way, I almost sensed that this was a challenge, to which I silently replied: "OK, lady, I'll show you!"

I considered these feelings and compared them to the way Sandy had made me feel about the same issue. I shouldn't compare, because I think the motivation was the same—caring. But, while I felt challenged with Caroline, I felt nagged with Sandy, and the more I am nagged, the less I respond positively. I think most people are like that. To be fair to Sandy, her nagging started when she knew me well. Caroline didn't know me that well when she made the statement, but I still didn't get the feeling that I was going to hear much on the subject again anyway. So I did it.

I was back at camp that Sunday night when I announced to all my band mates that I was giving up smoking. I couldn't have chosen a worse week to do it. The very next night, the captain decided to throw a Braai for us, and when we'd all finished eating, having drunk a few beers already, everyone pulled out their cigarettes and lit up. I don't know what got me through that night, as the cravings were enormous, but I managed that night...and the next...and the next.... and the one after that... And so on. I still wasn't out of the woods though. On our way to Joburg two weeks later, Nick Vlok wryly asked me how it was going. I told him that I was still holding up.

"Oh really? Let's see then. Light this for me..." Nick observed me closely, grinning slyly as I lit him a cigarette without inhaling the smoke, then passed it to him. I think he was genuinely impressed.

Caroline didn't seem to be: "You're not doing it for me, you're doing it for yourself." I do think though, that if I had caved and started again, she would have thought less of me, and that was something I wasn't going to let happen.

There are many feelings that flood young people infatuated with each other. Confidence, lust, admiration... And adventure. When you're starting to get to know a person on a romantic level, you find yourself asking a lot of questions. This is, fairly obviously, a natural part of the game of love. Most of the questions are easy to ask, but as you get to know someone more intimately, the excitement and sexual tension grows until you're led into that area where you know you're both taking a huge risk. But risks are for the bold, and in this case, I was as bold as a lion. Even then, I wasn't sure that the question that had been brewing in my mind would be answered in the affirmative, but I hadn't reckoned on the fact that Caroline was a girl who would not back down from a challenge. Whatever possessed me to ask the question, I don't know. I did know, however, that even though the request was hugely outrageous, if I crashed and burned I would rise from the ashes to ask a similarly outrageous question later on. With the benefit of hindsight, ours was never going to be a relationship that just fizzled and sputtered out like a fuse with no dynamite attached. I didn't realise it at the time, but I was in highly volatile territory.

We were coming back from the drive-in one night before I was due to go back to Kimberley (after yet another weekend pass), and as usual, the conversation was lively, interesting, and the mood was romantic.

I suddenly turned and said "Hey, why don't you come and spend a weekend with me in Kimberley? Any weekend!"

Long pause. "Are you being serious?"

"Definitely! It'll be fun."

Big grin, and a tentative "OK..., but how would we organise it? My dad would kill me if he found out!—Actually, he'd kill you!"

We laughed. This was very exciting stuff! Now we were on a roll. "Just tell him that you're going to stay with a friend or something." More grins and nervous laughter.

After discussing it casually for a bit longer, our attentions were turned to more pressing romantic issues, like how long could we hold our breath for while our tongues were down one another's throats... Seriously, I thought that was the end of the conversation, and didn't think much more about it.

I say I didn't think much more about it, but now that the subject had been raised, it crept into the back of my mind and hung around there, loitering with intent. The idea of a weekend away, just her and me, with no chaperones, was new territory for me. It would be like, well, serious stuff! Adult stuff! I was nineteen years old and Caroline was eighteen. We both realised the gravity of what I was proposing. This was not just graunching and fondling in the car, this was a couple of nights together, alone, about five hundred and fifty kilometres from our families! Sometime in the second week after we'd spoken I received a phone call from Caroline. Besides it being great to hear from her, I could sense that the conversation was leading up to something. Her tone became polite, but serious, with a hint of vulnerability in her voice:

"Clive, Do you still want me to come up to Kimberley?" (Uh Oh...) "I've spoken to my mom. She'll cover for us."

(Whaaat!!!) "Um, sure. I'd love you to come up." Hearing myself say that, for the first time since I'd raised the subject, I realised that we were now seriously getting down to business and I couldn't back down. After all, I wrote the cheque and she cashed it. Wow! This was really happening. Although I seemed hesitant at first, she knew that this was something I wanted. Was it for the sake of ego? Adventure? Dare I say it... Love? Whatever it was, we were both excited.

We then worked out that it would be best to "elope" around the second weekend of December, as Caroline was still in her final school year and would be finishing school and on holiday from the first week of December. The only thing I was really worried about was, were we going to be able to pull the wool over her dad's eyes? The prospect of spending an unfettered weekend with this rather magnificent creature and showing her off once again to my friends kind of made me less worried. So it was ego, then?! Maybe. We were both proud of each other, so that made sense at least, but it was by no means the whole story. This was to be a voyage of discovery.

IN THE MEANTIME...

——————◆◆——————

Back at camp, we didn't know it at the time, but our musical landscape was going to be changing. By December I had done three quarters of my National Service, and in some ways we had reached our peak as a team. We were still very popular and in-demand, and would remain so until the end of my tenure and beyond, but some personnel were going to be changing in January with the advent of new Roofs coming in. Before all that happened, however, we had Christmas and New Year to get through.

I decided to pay a visit to the Leonards and the Olszewskas the week before I went down to escort Caroline up for our weekend together, to wish them a Merry Christmas. At the Leonards, Sandy and I sat and filled in the gaps. The mystery of why she had split up with me was a deep as ever, with her telling me that when we had broken up was the time when she had the deepest feelings for me! By that time, however, I was quite over my heartache and was happily settling into a good solid friendship with her. In some ways I knew that it was more than that for her, but I was in a different headspace by then. The romantic and mysterious side of our relationship had not escaped me though, and with the trauma of our breakup, a song had begun to grow in my head. I started writing "November" fairly soon after we split up, and it was the week of my visit to Sandy that I played what I'd written to my band mates. I was flattered by their compliments, and the fact that Vincent in particular was impressed—so much so that he added a chord to my chorus that worked beautifully. It was a segue up to F major in the middle of the chorus that really enhanced the song and gave it momentum. We never performed the song as a band, but it became my first Seven Single, released by RAP records in 1981, enshrining my time in Kimberley and my romantic hopes with Sandy forever.

I was also learning a lot of new chords, both on piano and guitar, thanks to Vincent and John Ferrier. I had a good knowledge of guitar, but John was definitely more schooled in the art of rock and roll riffing than I was, and gave me some gems that I still use to this day. With the use of the band's Rhodes (a gift to Vincent from the Captain, as I mentioned earlier), I was working out chords that seemed to impress Vincent to the point of him showing me better ways to play them with different inversions. More importantly, I was discovering that I actually had a voice that people liked listening to, and that I could do interesting things with. This was quite an awakening for me, as vocals were always just something that I did as part of my overall musicality, and were second place to my efforts on guitar. In fact, for some reason, this side of my talent was getting some serious attention from the general public, which I admit did go to my head a bit, but for the first time in my life I realised that I could do something serious in music. I had written songs from the time I picked up a guitar, so that was not a new thing. What was new, was that I started realising that my songs were recordable and were starting to have a degree of maturity about them. I still regard this period of my life as a very positive time, from a songwriting perspective. And with Sandy dedicated in "November", my creative juices naturally flowed to my current romance with Caroline. The song came effortlessly and joyfully. "More Than The Other Girls" summed up my feelings so adequately about this new romantic adventure, that I experienced a sense of completion with a song that I'd never had before. While "November" was exciting and hopeful, "More Than The Other Girls" was peaceful and final. Music was becoming more and more vital in my "lifescape", and I knew then that my future was going to be seriously intertwined with it.

WITHOUT THE BLESSING
OF OUR FAMILY

———————◆◀———————

I have a dim recollection of the actual start of that fateful drive with Caroline up to Kimberley, but I remember the journey like it was yesterday! I met her at Uncle Charlie's Roadhouse South of Johannesburg on Friday at lunchtime, having hitchhiked down the previous afternoon, and we headed up to Kimberley in her car. I drove for most of the way, and halfway through our journey at a town called Wolmaranstad in the Northwest Cape, Caroline asked me to pull over. She went inside the grocery store and emerged with some drinks for us and some green apples and a small container of salt.

"Here, taste this..." she said laughing, quickly salting an apple and shoving it into my mouth, almost in one movement. I was taken completely by surprise and gagged at the combination of salt and sourness, but was pleasantly surprised by the aftertaste—as quite obviously was Caroline, French-kissing me to get the fullness of our tastebuds interacting. We did like to talk to each other. It was a very healthy relationship from a communication perspective. As the journey continued and it was getting darker, I decided that we should stay at a cabin that evening at a resort in Christiana, about an hour from Kimberley, just to break our journey. We were greeted by a jovial lady at reception who made us feel right at home. We had a memorable evening of necking and just enjoying each other's company, but no serious stuff just yet. It was a place that I would always remember for the complete contentment and anticipation of good times to come, and I daresay Caroline felt the same way. Was there anything better than this? The next day, we got up and continued our journey and got into Kimberley sometime late in the morning. I'd already selected a hotel, and the two of us booked in as Mr. and Mrs.

Let me take a moment here... I will never forget hearing myself say that for the first time in my life... "We'd like a room for ourselves—Mr. and Mrs. Hay"... It was absolutely surreal at the time and made me realise, however briefly, how serious it was to be married. To this day, I don't know if the lady who booked us in believed that we were married. To make matters worse, the two of us were trying desperately not to laugh, and failing in the process. I was seriously worried that she was going to ask us for some proof of marriage—neither of us was even wearing a ring!

Somehow though, we were ushered up the stairs to our room. Here we were then... Two young people playing husband and wife, and realising that this wasn't going to be a charade—this was the real thing! Just the two of us, lusty teenagers spending the night together, in a hotel room, far from our parents.

There was a mixture of nervousness and excitement, and I had to join the band for a gig at the Kimberley Sun that night. I was very happy to be escorting my stunning girlfriend, even though I was playing, because the gig was being held by the Young Lions and was therefore quite a classy affair—in the best function room that this newest hotel had to offer, and very well catered. We spent the afternoon wandering around Kimberley window shopping and doing some random sightseeing before heading back to our hotel to get ready for the night. Once we had changed (with me giving milady her privacy to conduct her transformation), we jumped into the Mazda and headed for the hotel.

All my team were there as well as some of Vincent's and we set up, tuned up and started playing. The evening was off to a good start, and during our first break we all got something to eat. Alan was chatting to Caroline with his typical unassuming charm (which made me a bit defensive) while I was getting some technical stuff done. I soon joined them all at the table and we finished eating and carried on playing. At one point, when one of the others were singing, I jumped off the stage and danced with Caroline in the hope that she would consider this a very romantic gesture. Apparently she did.

At evening's end, Mr. and Mrs. Hay jumped back into the car and headed back to our hotel.

Love is a serious business—not something to place in the hands of human beings. And yet, we humans are given the ability, opportunity and desire to exercise love on many levels. When we are young, sexual desire is the primary expression that is chosen to exercise it, and why not?! Discovery, excitement, conquest... These are all things that drive a young man and sometimes they are intertwined with real feelings that create confusion—and can lead to disaster if not dealt with delicately. We are all amateur tightrope walkers, hoping to make it to the other side of the rope without falling off. Very few actually make it to the end, while some go further than others, reaching deeper chasms before plummeting, and some attempts fail only a third of the way through...

I considered myself fairly adept in the knowledge of women's sexuality by the time I was nineteen. Don't get me wrong, I was no expert, but I had walked that tightrope before covering various distances. And I had got to the other side at sixteen years old, only to realise that I was way too young to put my future at risk by staying on the other side. I wanted to walk that tightrope again and again and again!!

I didn't immediately realise that this was all new to Caroline. She seemed so natural, and we worked so well together. When we got back to the hotel, without much further ado we got down to the business of love—and we walked that tightrope all the way! We fell asleep, woke again in the morning, and made love again, before getting up. Caroline was quiet. Too quiet. She got up, displaying her magnificent breasts before getting into the shower. This was one magnificent creature that I was balancing with, and it seemed that we had slipped on the metaphorical tightrope and were hanging in midair...

Breakfast was a quiet affair, and as we got into her car for the journey back to Johannesburg, things were definitely not right with us. The silence was deafening and awkward. This was going to be a long journey. We passed Christiana, but this time there was no joy, just a realisation that this girl wanted to get home. A little while after Wolmaranstad the tension finally broke and I pulled the car over as Caroline collapsed into my arms sobbing uncontrollably. We sat there as she finished crying and dried her tears. I felt helpless and hapless. All I could do was hold her—and I knew it wasn't enough. I was aware that she would have been somewhat sore, but I also had the horrible feeling that she felt that she had made a mistake by giving herself to me, and now there was no going back, and there was nothing either of us could do about it. Why? Was I such a cad? Hadn't we both known that this was going to happen between us? I didn't know the answer then, and I wasn't sure for a while afterwards.

We got back to Kempton and Caroline dropped me off at home, and returned with I don't know what story for her mother. What was her dad going to say about her crying? Surely he'd want to know what was going on? My mother, wise as ever, had suspected something was up when I got home. I didn't tell her much at all, but she could see that Caroline wasn't her old self when she dropped me off. I spent a couple of hours at home, ate, and was dropped off at the train station by my stepfather to go all the way back to Kimberley. By the time I got back to camp on Monday morning, I realised that I had just travelled roughly two thousand kilometres in forty eight hours for a roll in the hay! It was a weekend that will always be remembered for its joy, passion and heartbreak.

BUT NOW IT'S
UNRESOLVED... OR IS IT?

S o what now? I knew it wasn't over between us, but I also knew that things had changed. How much they had changed, I couldn't say. I found myself in a romantic no-man's-land. I even unburdened my troubles on Vincent and Diane, only to be told by a smiling but sympathetic Diane that Caroline was probably sore and uncomfortable right now, and that I must give it time. Vincent chimed in, quoting a Tom Petty song, with "Why don't you guys just 'Breakdown'?" Well, Vincent, we had. And I was hoping to fix the wreck. As for Diane's well-meaning advice, I kind of knew that already, but it was interesting hearing a woman's perspective, though I couldn't help analysing the crap out of the situation, and coming up with no satisfactory answers. I was in torment, and would once again torture the ears of my friends in a quest for advice on the workings of the female psyche. They also really didn't have a clue, so I decided I needed to go back to the source. I had been phoning Caroline in the week following, but instead of the carefree conversations we'd been used to, these were slightly stilted, and tinged with concern on my part. Guilt was hounding me, and I needed some kind of closure. I was getting to the stage where I needed to take some direct action, so I applied for two weeks leave over the Christmas period to: a) see where the land lay with us, and: b) try and repair the relationship.

I told my parents that I was coming home, and they were over the moon. It would be my first Christmas back at home in two years. The time dragged, but eventually, about two weeks later, I found myself hitch hiking my way back to Joburg. While it was great to catch up with my family again, it didn't escape my parents notice that this was only partly the reason why I had decided to spend the festive season at home. I was full of hope, however, and proceeded to phone Caroline the day after I got in to arrange time with her. This, it turned out, was suddenly not the cinch it had been before Le Weekend! We did go out on a few occasions, but I was hoping to do a whole lot more than go out, and hoping to spend a whole lot more time together than we did. Christmas came, and I went with my parents to my aunt and uncle's house South of Johannesburg. This was our ritual every year. My uncle had a large Spanish styled house in a fairly exclusive suburb right opposite a golf course, and at Christmas he lavishly entertained approximately sixty people every year, including some well known entertainment personalities, which was just up my alley. I was hoping for a happier Christmas, even with all the hoopla. I didn't have my girl with me, and I wasn't holding my breath too hard.

I was surprised therefore when she phoned me the next day and said she had a Christmas present for me. I don't recall if I'd bought anything for her, but I probably had, so this was an opportune moment to talk and see where the land lay.

Caroline arrived at my house late the next afternoon. After we'd greeted each other and she had spoken to my parents for a bit, we moved into my room. We sat on the bed and she kissed me and handed me a present. I really had no clue as to what it could be, so I opened it, expecting it to be a t-shirt or something that I would probably stop using after a short time. It turned out to be the latest Yes album, *Tormato* (I was a die-hard Yes fan), which I still have, somewhere in my old record collection. I was pretty knocked out with this, and proceeded to put it on my turntable and play it from beginning to end—in those days that's what we did with an album.

We went out later that night to the Drive-In, stopping later at a roadhouse to eat—no apples with salt this time—and I decided to try and find out what was going on in her head. I asked her how she was feeling. "Fine."

Oh-kay..." Listen, I'm sorry you were so upset when we left Kimberley. Are WE still ok?"

" Yes, but I don't think we should do THAT again..." Shy laughter.
"Why not—you're beautiful!"

"No..." More shy laughter. We moved off the subject and the conversation got lighter again and more along the lines of how we used to interact before Le Weekend. Although this was a good sign, when she dropped me off at home, she said "You know, when we talk like this I feel more like you're a great friend than anything else..." What?! I was gutted. Friend? This was code for a breakup—usually my domain!

With a mixture of pride and a drop in self-confidence, I asked "But what if I wanted to marry you?" I firstly couldn't believe my own ears, and secondly, I knew what the answer to that was before it even left those luscious lips. "We're way too young for marriage, and besides, I don't want to get in the way of your music career!"

"But by the time I'm established, you or I might both be married!"

"Well, then we'll have an affair!" came the callous reply.

I didn't sleep very well that night, and spent the next day trying to figure out how to spend the rest of my leave, which didn't seem to feature Caroline too much. She was right, of course. I was nowhere near ready for marriage, and if I was to be honest with myself, would I sacrifice the music career for a relationship that was currently this rocky? But I wasn't about to let honesty get in the way of my imagination, so I thought that somehow, we would be OK. I phoned Tommy Thompson to see what he was up to. He said he would come by that evening and we could go to The Boat. For the rest of the day I listened to records, read and had lunch with my mom, who suddenly threw me a curve ball...

"I'm not impressed with Caroline, Clive!" "Why?" I asked, dumbfounded! Not only was I extremely surprised by this statement, but I also felt somewhat vulnerable about the fact that my private life was being scrutinized by my mother!

"I know you took this time off to spend with her, and she's treating you pretty dismally. Look at you—you're miserable!" she said.

"It's not her fault mom," I replied in defense of the first woman who had ever had me in such a spin.

"It takes two to tango, my boy. You both knew what you were doing, and now you're being held at arm's length!" came the matter-of-fact reply.

I was embarrassed, and shocked all at once by this statement. How did my mom know about Le Weekend? In retrospect I must've been pretty naive thinking that my parents had no idea, but at that time, and with this last statement, my mother was someone who could see through walls, could read minds and knew a lot about everything.

It did get me thinking, though. I did realise that this relationship was becoming distinctly one-sided. But I also realised that there was a vulnerability about my girl that she didn't want to expose to me again in too much of a hurry. I had taken a piece of her heart that she could never retrieve. Was this love, though, for her to hold both her own, and my feelings at bay? After roistering about in the early part of the week with Tommy, Mally phoned me and asked me if I wanted to go to dinner at a restaurant on Wednesday night with Tracy, his girlfriend. I said yes, I'd love to, and would they mind if Caroline came along? "No problem," was the reply, so I phoned Caroline to see if she wanted to go. To my surprise, she said yes, but I had this awkward feeling that I was being done a favour.

The date was a date that will live in infamy... OK, let's not get too dramatic, but it was pretty bad. Mally and Tracy gave me a lift to Caroline's place, and we all got out of the car and went to the door. Caroline answered the door and I did the introductions. We all went inside the house, where her dad was holding court in the lounge, making thinly-veiled sarcastic comments in my direction, to which I politely laughed—he was joking, of course! We headed out the door and Caroline decided she wanted to drive.

Never put an angry woman in a driver's seat. For that matter, don't put her in the passenger seat either! Mally and Tracy followed in his car.

"How old is that girl with Malcolm?"

"Fifteen, I think."

"You mean we're double dating with one of Aimlee's friends?"

"I don't know..."

132

"That girl is the same age as my sister! I'm damned if I'm going to be socialising with one of my sisters friends!"

With that, she put her foot on the gas and drove away as fast as possible from Mally's car. I protested, to no avail. I was torn. On the one hand, my groin was talking and I didn't really care if we had lost Malcolm and Tracy. On the other hand, what kind of selfish behaviour was this?! This was one of my best friends. Who cared if his girlfriend was fifteen or thirty! I seriously thought of asking her to stop and drop me off. The problem was, we were in the middle of the freeway, miles from nowhere. Self preservation kicked in. Did I REALLY want to walk twenty kilometres back home? The journey continued, however, with alternating feelings of pleasure and betrayal. I felt compromised. What was I going to tell Malcolm? It was the Kevin scenario all over again, except this time, Mally was the one being left behind. At least he had a car! I vowed that when I got my license, I was NOT going to be put in this position again!

We got into Hillbrow, with no sign of Malcolm or Tracy around. Mally had booked the restaurant somewhere in town, and I had no idea where it was. We parked the car and sat.

"What are we going to do now?" I asked.

"We can go to movies at the Nu Metro cinemas here!" she replied.

"OK," I conceded.

The movie was Mel Brooks' *High Anxiety*. Not a great choice—a comedy full of sexual innuendo. Tension in the air, and not good tension!

The drive home was painful. I was searching her face for some kind of breakdown in feelings. None was forthcoming. She dropped me off at home and we said goodnight. I asked if I could see her before I went back to camp and she agreed, but this was not two lovebirds cooing here. I wandered off into the house, wondering whether I really wanted to continue like this...

YET THEY KNOW THAT
THEY'RE BOTH TO BLAME

———————◆◆———————

The next day, Mally phoned me and asked what had happened to us. I came up with some lame excuse, like we had got lost or something. I didn't want to insult one of my best friends by telling him that my girlfriend was a superior bitch who had decided that he and his girlfriend weren't good enough company for her. We went out that night with Tommy to a roadhouse and chatted and joked inanely. Tommy and his infectious laugh—always made me feel better. All the while though, my head was somewhere else. Mally and Tommy, while being two of the best friends a guy could have, weren't Agony Aunts of any kind. And whenever I ventured a question, or stated my current confusion, I was met with abrupt statements or jokey quips, leaving me frustrated. I decided to put my confusion on hold and just enjoy an evening with two great mates.

Friday rolled around, and with my leave coming to an end shortly, I decided to phone Caroline to ask her if we could get together on the Saturday. She agreed, and we spent the morning at a couple of shopping malls. Just after lunch, another nail got driven into our relationship coffin—I managed to reverse her car into a wall. The damage was not insignificant, but it wasn't major. Understandably, she was mad as hell! I don't know what was worse, my feeling of incompetence, or the stony silence that followed us back to my place. We said our goodbyes. She was leaving on Monday morning for a family holiday to Mauritius, and she said she needed time to pack and organise herself. I was due to head back to camp on the Monday as well. No one had said anything, but we both knew I was on a slippery slope here.

Looking back, maybe I shouldn't have been so hasty with my letter. But then again, I felt like I was a part-time lover in the court of Queen Caroline, waiting for her to beckon me when she felt the urge to be amused. A tad over-sensitive? Maybe, but things were not what they had been, and, not being one to overstay my welcome, I decided to bow out as discreetly as I could, without too much fuss. I really thought this would be a welcome move, with milady shedding a small tear for my benefit, but exhaling a silent breath of relief at my departure. I honestly was under that impression. I couldn't have been more wrong.

That Sunday afternoon, on the eve of Caroline's holiday, and the eve of my return to Kimberley, I sat down and composed my letter of departure, which said, in effect, "Thank you for everything, but we should go our separate ways. Hopefully we can meet under better circumstances in the future when we're both mature enough to commit to one another, I'll never forget you," etc, etc.

I must admit, I was angry with her, having been in her ample bosom, being caressed and loved in such a way as to make me feel like there were only the two of us in the world, and then being reduced to an understudy, waiting in the wings to be called out at the producer's whim. I had had enough. It was 6pm. I picked up the phone and called her. I told her I wanted to see her before she went.

"I'm busy packing," she replied...

My voice was commanding: "I want to see you before you go. I have something for you."

Sensing my insistence, she relented, and I got hold of Clifton and asked him to come over. He was somewhat bewildered by my sudden interest in his company, until I asked him if we could hang out at his place, but could we please swing by Caroline's place first. Knowing that we were an item, and perhaps wanting to enhance our friendship, however, he happily did my bidding. When we got there, I had a somewhat déjà vu moment when Caroline came out to meet me, smiling that beautiful smile, and looking quite gorgeous. It reminded me of Sandy's ultimatum and my subsequent visit to her, inveigling me with her charms, which, while effective in the short term, led to our eventual downfall. In the present moment, it seemed that Caroline quite liked this Devil May Care attitude that I was displaying when I handed her my letter. I was acting fairly distant, which only seemed to pique her interest some more. She smiled playfully.

"Are you OK?"

" I'm fine, thank you," I said, somewhat aloof.

"What's in here?" came the curious inquiry.

"Read it later. Have a great holiday."

She laughed half-quizzically and half-teasingly. "OK" she smiled. She kissed me goodbye. It was the second-last kiss I ever got from her.

The saying goes "Hell hath no fury like a woman scorned". In my short life, I had never been on the receiving end of this fury, mainly because if I broke up with any girl before I met Caroline, it was always met with tears and sorrow, and perhaps a few bitchy comments. Not fury.

Clifton, as I had mentioned, lived a few hundred metres up the road from Caroline. No sooner had we set foot in the door than Clifton's mother, who I had met maybe once before, emerged and told Clifton that Caroline was on the phone for me. Sensing what the phone call would be about, and feeling a mixture of pride and relief that I had delivered my message, I was expecting subdued tones and recriminations. I couldn't have been more wrong. Without going into too much detail, I can liken myself to a fire fighter, trying desperately to stem a roaring blaze on my own, that I myself had started—and failing miserably. I was on the phone to Caroline for an hour. Clifton's mother kept on yelling at Clifton to get me off. I wasn't moving. But I also wasn't getting a word in edgewise. I was threatened, cajoled, denigrated and mocked, all through hysterical screaming, full of tears. What on earth was happening here? Did this girl actually have feelings for me after all, or was she just extremely angry because she had been dumped? I knew that I had feelings for her, but I wasn't happy to be playing on the sidelines of her life either. All I could squeeze in amongst the tirade was a few feeble I love you's, which were met with a mixture of tears and mocking laughter. When I did finally raise my voice in protest, it was met with bitter one-liners and counter-accusations. There was no leaving the premises whole. We ended our conversation after Clifton's mother threatened to unplug the phone from the wall. And there it was—the bitterest of ends. She had cried for the better part of an hour. I wondered what on earth her parents would be thinking, as such a tirade surely wouldn't have escaped their attention. Sad and dejected, the next day I headed back to camp. I bored Alan and Dave to tears with my story, but in effect, I had resigned myself to the fact that this was over, and this girl hated me and wanted nothing more to do with me. Wrong again. About a week later I got a card in the mail. Recognising Caroline's handwriting I cautiously opened it. Now, to give you some idea, Caroline's letters before Le Weekend were eagerly anticipated. They were beautifully crafted and written, with always that promise of romance and mutual anticipation of hearing from and seeing one another. She always sprayed them with her perfume, whose aroma made me weak at the knees and see imaginary love hearts in front of my eyes.

This was different. It was a card, sent from Mauritius. It said: "Is Cupid stupid, or is he just a bad shot?" She had written a message to me on the inside. "Dearest Clive, still thinking of you at four in the morning". I received two more such letters with short but similar sentiments, which really had me confused. After all that, did this girl really care for me? I was filled with hope.

Einstein himself said it: What do women want? Personally, I don't know, but I'm pretty sure that men can't adequately provide whatever it is they want. One phone call to Caroline clinched that for me. After these letters from her stating her love, heartbreak and bitterness, I foolishly thought that I had done her a grave wrong, and that only my guilty verbal recompense might bring us back together. So I phoned her. Was she happy to hear from me? Decidedly not. Was she going to milk this situation for as long as possible and make me grovel? You betcha!

Now, with the benefit of many years behind us and a renewed friendship with this very special girl, all of this seems fairly silly behaviour from both of us. At the time, though, I thought she was somewhat cruel for not giving me the chance to explain and redeem myself, and perhaps even redeem the relationship. Truth be told, my mind (and probably my groin) was telling me that I might be ready for something serious, but I knew in my heart that, right then, I wasn't! I guess I wanted to expunge myself of whatever guilt I thought I had, thereby having my cake and eating it too. She wasn't about to let that happen though, and foolishly, I let this behaviour continue for awhile instead of just saying c'est la vie sooner rather than later, and allowing both of us to get on with our lives. As it was, the phone calls became less frequent, and seeing as they never ended well, or ended inconclusively, I finally gave up and moved on from an unresolved situation. She was getting on with her life anyway, it seemed; and I was becoming more of a nuisance than anything else. It was a sad way to end what had been an incredible four month journey together, and I never forgot the first time I had met my match and how I let it burn right down to my fingers.

As a post-script, I mentioned earlier that when I dropped off the fated letter, I received my second-last kiss from Caroline. The last time she kissed me was some two years later. I was busy making a name for myself around Joburg as a musician and had just recorded my first single, "November". Clifton threw a party at his house to which I was invited, and hearing that Caroline might be there, I decided to go. We were still barely on speaking terms and I hadn't seen her for a while, so I was somewhat filled with trepidation when I arrived. I had also brought a casual date with me as backup in case I was going to be left standing around like a lost fart in a perfume factory.

No sooner had I entered than I was accosted by a smiling Caroline who, in front of my date, grabbed me and French-kissed me until I could barely breathe. I introduced her to the girl I was with, and later used the opportunity to try and get to grips with our unresolved issues. At first she was playful and friendly, which made me think of the old days, but as we carried on talking, a sadness and almost a defeated look came over her, and she cast her face down. I knew then that there was still something that I had stolen from her heart that could never be returned. But whatever piece of her heart I had, she surely must have known that she still had a piece of mine...

SILVER TAINTS THE SKY

I returned to camp a different person in some ways. The seriousness of life was starting to creep in. This was not a bad thing. Just
different. I had six months left in the army and I guess I knew that
I had some serious life decisions to make going forward. One of them
would be what I decided to do for a career going forward. After leaving school, in the six months before I went into the army, my mother
had got me a job at Barclays Bank. One of the reasons she wanted
me working there was that they paid me a monthly stipend while I
was doing my national service. There were no conditions attached,
which suited me because the last thing I wanted to be was a banker,
and I knew that as soon as I was in a position to do so, I would exit
that profession. In the meantime, my last six months were destined
to be almost as full as the past twelve months . The memory of Caroline still lingered like a shadow, however, making that last passage
of time in the army, and all my subsequent adventures in and around
Kimberley, a strange concoction of bittersweet experiences. But the
strength and purpose of my future career choice would be strongly
forged in this last hurrah before the world and all its complexities hit
me.

For starters, the captain was removed from his position as
company commander and, by default, removed from direct
responsibility over the band. And gigs, though still coming in, were
not very plentiful that January. Both Hughie and I were removed
from our positions as company clerks and we kicked around in
various other jobs before I managed to wangle myself a position in
the roneo room with a very pleasant guy by the name of Rob, an
Eastern Province Rugby player. Rob and I were a law unto ourselves.

141

As long as we did our job of making copies of various official papers, nobody bothered us. That is, until one day when I discovered a piano in the next room... But more of that later.

The new year started off innocently enough with us doing New Year's Eve at the Alarm Clock, a restaurant belonging to Karen De Lange's dad. It was one of the best and most sought after places for dining out in Kimberley, being ensconced in the Trust Bank building, one of the newer and taller buildings in town. Because I had taken Christmas off, Vincent was going home for New Year, and seeing that one of us had to be there to oversee things, my band got the gig. I asked Vincent if we could use his PA for the night, it being newer and less cumbersome than the army one. He agreed with some reservation. Pete Auths decided that I should ask for his Echoplex as well. I was fairly reluctant to do so, seeing as I wasn't sure how to use it properly and we had a fairly decent Echo unit anyway, but Pete was insistent, so I relented and asked. Vincent was starting to get antsy. It was one thing asking for the PA—now we wanted his Echo unit as well?! He relented anyway, and we were ready to see in the New Year for the expected crowds.

Except there were no crowds. This was Kimberley, and anyone who didn't have to be there over the Christmas and New Year celebrations wasn't. They were in better locations like Cape Town, East London, PE, Durban or, dare I say it, Mauritius.

From the start, Karen's dad was not pleased with the turnout and was looking for a scapegoat. It was us. It was bad enough playing to approximately ten people, but to have the owner scowling as he walked past the stage was something else. Then we hit a problem. Even though we had the Echoplex, I hadn't used it that evening until Pete begged me to turn it on. I wasn't that au fait with the settings, so I declined. Pete insisted, so on it went, if only to teach him a small lesson.

The song was Billy Joel's "Just the Way You Are", and it was hilarious! Poor Pete. The Echoplex was connected to the Rhodes that Pete was playing, and all the notes that emanated from it when Pete played were doubled and crossed over each other. I was in fits and could barely sing, which didn't help our situation with Mr. De Lange. The same thing happened with the next song, at which point I decided to turn the Echoplex off. To compound my mirth, Pete had written down the set list that we were busy with, and he'd written the next number as "Lion Eyes" (i.e "Lyin' Eyes" by the Eagles). Then, to make matters worse, Dave Oldham had brought with him the beautiful Deolinda, her brother and his girlfriend. The brother was an absolute piece of work, and his girlfriend wasn't much better. They both proceeded to get drunk and aggressive—never a good combination—with Dave and Deolinda trying as politely as possible to get them to calm down. This time it was "Poor Dave", who, not being too assertive, but known to speak his mind, was drowned out by abusive epithets and shouts from Deolinda's brother such as "I'm from Joburg. Don't mess with me, ekse!!" What an idiot. By the time twelve o' clock came, whatever patrons there were had thinned out, leaving us with less than a handful of people to sing "Old Lang Syne"' to. Then came the bombshell. Our host decided in his wisdom that he hadn't made enough money to pay the band! I protested, to no avail. The boys all stood around wondering what to do. Eventually we left, deciding to fight another day.

On the following Monday when Vincent got back we had a meeting with the captain (who, at that stage, had not yet relinquished his post) about how to handle this turn of events. To be honest, we weren't that worried about the situation. Who would, when you have the government on your side?! It was decided that four of us should go and politely request what was owing to us once again, so Vincent, Ian, Eddie and I jumped into a car and headed for the Alarm Clock. We got there around 11am and found Mr. De Lange at the front desk. He immediately got defensive when he saw us. We requested our funds as politely as possible, to which he replied in the negative, because, as he put it, "There were no F$&@*#en people here!!" After which he proceeded to order us out of his shop. We weren't going anywhere without the money, and Ian, to his credit, started threatening him with the military police if he didn't pay up! That got the required response, but we were ordered out of the

Alarm Clock, never to return. I wasn't sure exactly how this affected Vincent's secret affair with Karen, but to be honest, that was the last thing on my mind right then.

Change was in the air. While some of it was inevitable, sometimes we were pleasantly surprised, and in one case it came from a most unexpected source. In all the time we had been playing, the powers that be demanded that we fork over half of our earnings, which was allegedly put into a band fund for the purposes of buying new gear or any other expenses that we might need. Seeing as we didn't have a say in this, we just assumed that the leadership were frittering away half of our hard-earned pay on drink, new clothes for their wives, or other personal activities. Also, with the demise of the captain's position over us and the very tenuous position we were in, we weren't expecting anything! Guess what?! That's right—they'd actually kept the money in the fund, and to boot, they'd bought Magirus a Band Bus! Now never mind that this bus was in a very shaky state of repair; we now had our own wheels! No more requisitioning Bedfords from the Transport Park, sitting in the back and freezing our tails off at two in the morning hundreds of kilometres from base. This thing had seats and we all sat together—very civilised. Another change that wasn't so good was that Kaffirtjie had asked for, and was given, authority over a marching band—and Alan, James and Willie Els were press-ganged into it. This was going to be a rather large source of friction between my old nemesis and myself. Practice times and gigs would clash, and with him hating me as much as he did, as well as him being a sergeant major and myself being a lowly lance-corporal, I foresaw problems ahead.

Back to Dave and Deolinda. While my love life was in a mess, theirs seemed to be very strong indeed. Dave, Alan, Pete and I hung out a lot together and I would often find myself with Dave at Deolinda's place, with me being a rather interested spectator to their violent bouts of couch rugby. They would throw each other all over her bedroom, laughing, then kissing, then wrestling, all the while whispering sweet nothings. I didn't mind, but witnessing all this canoodling did make me feel a bit forlorn. Their behaviour had quite a serious downside, as I was later to discover. One thing did cheer me up that January—I passed my drivers license—first time! What was it with me and my license? It was always preceded by a dramatic breakup. Maybe that wasn't such a bad thing. Maybe it made me more determined to pass. I don't know, but as I stood before the test officer at the end of my drive, too nervous to ask whether I'd passed or not, I felt a twinge of gratitude towards my exes. An older man was standing nearby.

" Did you pass?"

"I don't know..." I half whispered.

"Man, ask the officer," he said in a kind, but insistent way.

(Nervously, not wanting to really hear if it was bad news) "Excuse me Officer, did I pass?"

(Looking up from his paperwork with a scowl) "Just!!"New found freedom! No more relying on anyone to ferry me around at an inconvenience to them. Now all I needed were some wheels of my own. Scouring the Diamond Fields Advertiser, I came across two possibilities within an acceptable (and affordable) price range: one was a Toyota Bakkie (utility vehicle) for R1200, and the other was a VW Kombi panel van for R900. Being a mere Teenage National Serviceman, the price made my mind up for me, and soon Dave Oldham and I were heading off to a location near Sandy's place to negotiate a deal. The problem was, I didn't have R900 to spare and would have to convince the owner that I was a good risk to pay the vehicle off. I had R150 for a down payment and then would have to appeal to his sense of trust to pay the rest off over the six months I had left. I arrived at the house with a sense of nervous hopefulness, and Dave and I were ushered to the driveway where the car stood. She was a beauty—light blue, with a perfect engine and enough space to give ten troopies a lift home, and, should I have a date, fool around nicely in the back without being seen. I put my plight to the owner—a swarthy man with a gruff, yet gentle manner. He was not happy. He would rather sell the car for cash! He had been ripped off before when, in good faith he made a similar arrangement with someone. I assured him that I was as good as my word, and that I'd be in Kimberley for awhile yet... He looked me over and made me promise to honour our agreement then got me to sign a document to pay the rest over six months. I willingly signed, he handed me the keys, and Dave and I drove back to base. I was over the moon!

One of the first gigs I did using my new wheels as transport was at the Kimberley City Hall. It was quite a big affair so we pulled out the big guns for it, with full brass—Alan, James and Willie Els; three keysmen—Pete, Vincent and Huey; two drummers—Eddie and Nick; Dave on bass guitar and Ferrier and I on guitars, with a range of us sharing vocal duties. Dress was our red shirts and extremely tight black pants. It was a fairly pedestrian affair except for one incident, hence the mention of our dress code.

One of our first numbers was Elton John's "Love lies Bleeding", a song particularly close to my heart at that time. But that night, feeling confident, I put down my guitar and moved out front to do the lead vocal. The minute I had moved, I had Ferrier moving in yelling something at me. Typical, I thought—always trying to steal the limelight. Again he moved in, yelling something at me. I decided to ignore it, staring confidently at the rather gorgeous blonde and her boyfriend dancing in front of me, and carried on singing—no-one was going to steal MY thunder!! I got through the first verse and chorus and was getting lots of smiles from the punters. "This is GREAT!" I thought. As the eight bar interlude played, with me feeling like I'd missed my calling as a frontman, I decided to turn rather patronisingly to John and lend him my ear. He sauntered up to me again, and this time I heard him loud and clear: " Your fly's down!"...

A MEMORABLE WEEKEND

As I mentioned earlier, a lot happened in that last six months, and most of it related to my musical development. But towards the end of January, some of us got the opportunity to have a weekend off, so Dave invited Vincent, Hugh, Pete, Ferrier, James, Alan and myself to his house in Queenstown. We decided to leave straight after lunch, around 2pm on the Friday, travelling in two cars for the seven hour journey down there. It was quite novel having Vincent around, as we never saw him outside camp—he was either at Diane's or Karen's place. I was the only one privy to the information about Karen, as he had confided in me earlier. We made a merry crew on the way down, stopping for a bite at the Wimpy outside Bloemfontein as the sun began to set. After our meal, we resumed our trip, our conversation peppered with joyful anecdotes about our Christmas and New Year's holidays, mixed in with the anticipation of being in a new part of the world (I for one had never been to the Eastern Cape before, let alone Queenstown). I was travelling with James, Vincent and Hugh, and as the journey progressed, I nodded off, only to be awakened by the movement of the car through the Eastern Cape mountains. I was impressed. As we negotiated our way around the bends of the pass, the shadows of the bergs loomed like huge dark, jagged sentinels, silently witnessing our lives, as we would witness a wayward insect weaving its way around a kitchen floor, knowing that its life was in the eye of the beholder. When I verbally expressed my awe to James, his response was "If you want to see mountains, go to Cape Town!"

We rolled into Queenstown at about 11pm and filed into Dave's house. We were met by his dad, a short, bespectacled and friendly, somewhat opinionated man in his fifties. Dave's mom was asleep, so after an initial catch-up with his dad, we all crashed out—wherever we could find a spot. Some of the boys were lucky to get a bed. I got the couch—comfortable enough, but more comfortable for me was the camaraderie of our friendship, knowing that we were all together having the time of our lives! The next morning, we awoke to find that Dave's mom had prepared a delicious breakfast for us, after which we all headed into the town centre to check out what this sleepy little town had to offer. Dave assured us that it was by far preferable to life in a big city, and that people didn't even have to lock their doors at night! As we walked through the town, Dave and I separated from the group and the subject of Deolinda suddenly arose. He was eager to talk. Knowing him as I do now, he is something of a hopeless romantic, but nothing prepared me for how serious he was taking this relationship. He told me how in love he was with her, and that they should get married. I nearly tripped. I have to say here in Dave's defense that I've never been the most sensitive soul when it comes to people divulging their feelings to me, especially when I think they've taken leave of their senses.

"What?"

"I want to marry her, Clive, and soon!"

"Dave, you're nineteen years old! How are you going to support her?"

"I'll find a job. I reckon I'll be able to support her."

"But you've still got another year left of your national service. You could never support her on what they pay NSM privates, Dave."

"I'm telling you, we'll be OK!"

I was starting to get pretty annoyed at this pie in the sky talk, and I upped my diatribe. "You're off your head, Dave! I've never heard such unrealistic bullshit in my life!"

It was only obvious to me later, on a visit to Deolinda and her parents soon after I'd left the army myself, that I wasn't reading between the lines of Dave's outpourings of romanticism. Apparently the name Dave Oldham was not held in high esteem in the Fourie household. As a matter of fact, when I mentioned how sad I was that things hadn't worked out between them, and what a great couple I thought they made, both parents looked at me in disgust! I was puzzled. What was wrong? Was it an English/Afrikaans thing? Did Dave borrow money and not pay it back? Did he dump her for another girl? When they told me he had got Dee pregnant and she had to have an abortion, I could scarcely believe it! But everything then fell into place for me with our conversation in Queenstown. Poor guy. He didn't deserve their wrath, and here he was a year earlier, trying to tell me in a roundabout way how much trouble he was in, and I wasn't hearing him. He must've been going through mental torture. But on that Saturday morning in Queenstown, I was just listening to a friend who I thought had just crossed over the border into the lunatic fringe.

After our tour of Queenstown that morning, Dave's dad informed us that we were all going to accompany him to Gonubie Beach in East London on Sunday—another first for me, as I'd never been to East London. As Dave was going to be spending the remainder of the day with his family, Hugh decided that we should steal a march on Dave and his parents, and head down to East London, some two hours from Queenstown, late that Saturday afternoon. Hugh had arranged for us to stay over at his girlfriend's parents house that Saturday night, a palatial domicile overlooking that very beach (Dad was a doctor and very wealthy). I'd met Hugh's girlfriend, a strikingly gorgeous brunette by the name of Antoinette, some months previously when she visited Hugh in Kimberley. We struck up a great friendship and were very fond of each other. Hugh was always the gentleman around her and took all this in his stride, even though I know he must have felt slightly peeved by her fondness for me, so I was very careful not to overstep the boundary with our mutual attraction. Besides, in some ways, I felt she was a bit out of my league, and I certainly wasn't going to jeopardise my friendship with Hugh. It was part of our unspoken code that girlfriends were out of bounds!

Hugh had earlier confided in me that Antoinette herself had fallen pregnant and had an abortion, and had been through a bad bout of depression as a result. What I couldn't figure out was whether or not he, or someone else, had been the perpetrator. They didn't have an easy relationship, but then again, I could relate easily to that, and Hugh and I would often pour our hearts out to each other regarding our women.

That night proved to be somewhat of an epiphany for me, as I shall explain: John, Vincent and the rest of our entourage, (with the exception of Hugh, who had decided to spend time with Antoinette and her folks), decided to check out the nightlife around East London. At one stage of the evening, our travels brought us to the Holiday Inn, where a very lively one-man-band by the name of Charlie Bates was plying his trade. Vincent and I were in hysterics at his rendition of Billy Joel's song "My Life" – not because he was doing it badly, but because of his gruff delivery of the song title words, "Myyy Life!!!"

Then, almost fatefully, Vincent turned and said to me: "You know Clive, we laugh at the likes of Charlie Bates thumping out these songs, but these solo musos make more money than almost anyone else on the music circuit." It was a line that I would not forget when I first set my foot on the road to earning a living from music, and advice that I remembered when I got my first gig as a solo entertainer.

After a fair night's sleep at Antoinette's folks place, we all wandered down to the beach to have a swim and hook up with Dave and his family before grabbing breakfast. I got a great deal of enjoyment watching Dave and his three older brothers interact. They all spoke with that flat, clipped Eastern Cape English accent, which amused me, being a Durban boy myself and growing up with similar tones. Interestingly, with the amount of time I'd spent in Kimberley speaking a lot more Afrikaans than I normally would, I wound up somewhat more guttural in my speech—a habit that took me a while to shake! Back to the brothers though, it had been quite a few years since they'd all been together, and apparently this meeting was going to be the last for a while as well. And so, accompanied by the beautiful Antoinette, who had met us at the beach, we decamped to her parents house for lunch, leaving Dave and his family a few hours to themselves.

It was one of those memories that has stayed with me vividly for all these years. A sumptuous lunch followed by John, Vincent and I going into the lounge of this massive house and finding a grand piano. We asked Antoinette if we could play, and soon I was launching into "Honesty" by Billy Joel. The three of us sat there swapping songs, and then John sent my emotions awry by suddenly playing "Lost without your Love" by David Gates. I was floored and transported back a few weeks to the love I had loved and lost so helplessly and haplessly. When and how he'd learnt it I have no idea, but he played and sang it beautifully. My enduring memory is of John and I sitting at the piano together and Vincent leaning on it to our left, John showing me the chords, and the three of us harmonising the chorus together. We soon attracted an audience, and we were only too happy to show off for whoever would lend an ear. Antoinette invited me to sit with her at the large bay window overlooking the beach, where we made small talk about the band. I asked her how things were with Hugh, as there had been some tension earlier. She became somewhat downcast, but seemed to want to confide in me. We covered some ground about their relationship, but nothing too deep, and finally Hugh joined us and they both treated themselves to a small counselling session that seemed to clear the air somewhat. I was rewarded with a huge hug and kiss from Antoinette and a slap on the back from Hugh.

Later, on the way back down to the beach, Antoinette had bought three cool-drinks, one of which she gave to Hugh. As I was standing with the others she approached me and put the one drink in my hand. As I quietly protested that there weren't enough to go around, she closed my hand over the bottle with hers, smiling her gorgeous smile and saying, "Oh no, this is for you—you're my favourite!"

THE MACLEARS, THE
NEW BLOODS AND THE
KIMBERLEY SUN KERFUFFLE

s I've said, I don't know what it is about me, but people
often feel they need to tell me their deepest and darkest
secrets. I was slowly beginning to realise this when Ian
decided that I was the right person to confide in about his latest
Amore. Her name was Sharon Maclear and we had been introduced
to her family by Malcolm, who had met her dad while flying radio
controlled aeroplanes—he and Malcolm were hobbyists. Like most
families then, they were very welcoming of NSMs like our band of
brothers, and soon we were a regular fixture at their house. Sharon
was an attractive redhead with large brown eyes, who seemed quite
particular in her choice of men. I was not included in that choice,
which bothered me a little—only because, like most guys, I prefer to
have the right of refusal and not the other way round! Not a biggie—I
definitely preferred blondes, as my taste up till then had made plain.
But I must say, her choice of Ian surprised me. Even more so, Ian's
choice of her surprised me! I was under the impression that he
preferred Bloemfontein girls-and Afrikaans ones at that! "Begin
liewe onderste as bo" he once told me, quoting a lover he had at
University in Bloem. He was into feet. If a girl had bad feet or toes in his
estimation, he would not pursue the relationship. Sharon obviously
passed with flying colours, and was seeking a teacher in the art of
love. Ian was happy to oblige, and was not remiss in furnishing me
with the details. At one of our gigs, Ian brought her along. I pointed
out to Alan that this was Ian's new girlfriend, to which he replied

"Oh, I thought a cow had just walked into the room", (referring to her enormous brown eyes).

The Maclear home was a refuge from our regular routine, as enjoyable as that routine was—we were still the kings of the castle, almost a principality unto ourselves. But there was still that homely feeling missing, a void that the Maclears and, toward the end of my tenure, the Drakes filled. John and I would sit in hysterics watching the Battle of the Bands on TV, enjoying the antics of Robin Auld in his fledgling days with the Lancaster Band, copying Angus Young, the guitarist from AC/DC, complete with school uniform, cap and satchel, shyly leaping from the stage. I reckon we could have beaten them all hands down! Malcolm and Reg would return from flying their planes, a pastime I must tell you that was as interesting as watching paint dry if you weren't in control of the plane. Mrs. Maclear was a pleasant and hospitable hostess, and Sharon's sister was a lovely kid, though she hadn't quite captured my heart as Valerie, Glynis' little sister, had.

Back in the music room two new names had surfaced: Malcolm du Plessis and Aubrey Boltman. Aubrey was an accomplished keys man who had started doing some gigs with us and who was slowly getting more ensconced with the band. A quiet person, he sadly passed away in his thirties. But at that time he was a growing presence on our radar. Malcolm was something of an accomplished keyboard player/ musical director/arranger who would soon be making a name for himself in our camp, and eventually take over the duty of overseeing the band, which was slowly moving in a different direction. Another person who was making his presence felt was Themi Venturas, a guitarist and singer who was also an accomplished actor. He would join us on the occasional gig, playing percussion or guitar, before moving into a more permanent role in Supertroop, the band that followed Magirus. These were the new bloods who would continue the proud Magirus tradition, albeit in a much more controlled environment than we had—the PF's finally had a handle on how to control this musical animal in their midst and they weren't going to let the new guys get away with what we got away with!

About that same time, I found myself at a loose end one night roaming the streets with Vincent. I found it very interesting that the person who had inspired me to AWOL in the first place actually had precious little experience in the art of being brazen about it. What I hadn't realised was that although Vincent AWOL-ed every night, it was almost always to Diane's place, where he stayed until all hours before going back to camp. Apart from gigs, he had virtually no experience of being out on the town in AWOL mode. Myself and some of the others, however, were seasoned veterans and familiar faces at a lot of the venues. It was with some surprise, therefore that when I suggested a visit to the Kimberley Sun Hotel, one of our locals, the normally fearless Vinny started back-pedalling!

"What are you doing?"

"Going in for a drink....!?"

"We can't go in there! It'll be crawling with PF's!"

"Ah, come on. It'll be fine!"

"This is crazy, Clive!! If we get caught here we'll be in so much shit!!"

"Come on Vince, it's getting late..."

A very reluctant and nervous Vincent followed me into the hotel, and in we walked—straight into a nest of our unit's national service officers sitting at a table; one of them was 2nd Lieutenant Graham Kershaw, the unit's adjutant, or law officer!! I heard a groan and some very nervous "I told you so's" behind me.

"What are you guys doing here?", asked a visibly surprised Graham Kershaw.

I decided that confidence was the best policy. Luckily, most of the loots with Graham knew about our lifestyle and weren't as surprised as our Adj.

"Having a drink!?"

"What do you mean 'having a drink'? Clive, you know you guys aren't allowed out of the camp! I can't sit here while you guys are out, I have to call the MP's..."

"Graham, we'll go into the other bar. You won't even know we're here!" (By this time Vincent was about to start foaming at the mouth...)

Suddenly, support from an unexpected quarter. "Come on Graham, leave them alone, man..." a couple of the other loots chipped in.

"OK, just make sure I don't see you, otherwise it's MY neck!!"

"Thanks Graham."

A visibly shaken and pissed off Vincent followed me into the bar. I was very relaxed. Graham's tone had been threatening, but never fatal. And I knew he didn't want to look like a killjoy in front of the other officers—even if he WAS the Adj!

"Ya-ah, you see what happens, Mr. Hay!"

"Vincent, it's fine. Did you REALLY think he was going to arrest us?"

"Ya, well, he could've if he wanted to, and then where would we be??"

I decided to let it go at that. After all, in spite of my bravado I was somewhat surprised at Graham's response. Didn't he know about our unspoken mutual agreement with the powers that be that allowed us free reign over this, our temporary dominion?? Very uncool, Graham!!

A QUICK TRIP TO PRETORIA

E arly in February, Vincent and I were called into the major's office and assigned a rather (for the two of us anyway) unusual task. We were to escort a prisoner who was a notorious AWOL-er to the army prison in Pretoria. This was a somewhat trepidacious task, for me anyway, with an enormous amount of responsibility. What if he escaped? I think both Vincent and I were aware that our reputations were on the line here. The one thing about the assignment that appealed to both of us, however, was that the prison was right opposite the entertainment corps, the real music Mecca for musicians in the army. My good friend Peter Hall (remember the going to Pretoria/NOT going to Pretoria fiasco at the beginning of this book?) had managed to wheedle his way in there early in our service, to my eternal jealousy. Little did I know that Vincent was going to use this opportunity to get himself ensconced there in a few short weeks. When it happened, I wasn't too envious. By the time he was transferred, I only had four months left in the army anyway, and had my own accomplishments, achieved in that time, to be proud of.

In the meantime, we had a prisoner to transfer.

He turned out to be a rather skinny, shifty sort who talked too much. Vincent, myself and our charge ordered lunch at Kimberley station; two burgers for the charge and me, and a pie and gravy for Vincent. I loved our train rides in South Africa—they were always sleepers with four bunks in blue leather and wooden panelling. The conductor would come knocking with the familiar monologue, "kaartjies asseblief/tickets please", and later on in the evening, usually after supper in the dining car, we would return to our car to find our beds made and turned down. We didn't truly realise it then, but we lived a privileged life in South Africa. We would be lulled to sleep by the clickety clack of the train, waking up at 2am to find ourselves in some tiny railway town, the conductor crying the all clear and blowing his whistle before we were rocked back to sleep by the slow movement of the train pulling out of the station.

This particular ride found us pulling into Pretoria at about 8am, where we were met by two MP's and escorted to the prison to hand our guy over. The prison was an interesting place, a lot more friendly than I thought it might be, with a lot of guys doing time for being conscientious objectors than real criminals. Conscientious objectors were kids who chose not to do national service out of the conviction that they didn't agree with government policy. That, or they were just too nervous about doing national service, which I found ridiculous, due to the fact that they wound up in prison for three years when they would be out in two if they just got it over with. Anyhow, with our duty duly served by 10am, we were free to spend the day as we pleased before catching the train back to Kimberley that evening at 6pm.

Needless to say, our first stop was the Entertainment Unit which was right across the road from the prison. It was almost like a homecoming, and it was great to see a few familiar faces and meet some new ones. Pete was particularly pleased to see me, as we had started out in Kimberley together and been separated by that initially cruel double decision four months into our service, that had me going to Pretoria on the Thursday, and then being sentenced to two years in Kimberley on the Friday. As you can see, I made the best of that sentence. Pete and I remain lifelong friends. Shortly after leaving the army we got a band together, called "Savannah", which kept us busy for two years before he moved into advertising, and finally the world of art. I sat in on a rehearsal with Pete's band and introduced Vincent to everyone I knew. There were a couple of guys who Vincent introduced me to who were real players as well, and who I would perform with a couple of times later on in my career. Looking back, I was unsure whether he was using this opportunity to try and wangle his way in, or whether or not he had organised things earlier. It wasn't really important—we were both enjoying the moment. Having finished our visit, we headed into town to watch a movie. What made that memorable was both of us emerging from the cinemas and me being bawled out by a colonel for not having my beret on. I made the mistake of answering him back when he brought it up. Apart from that, duty done, we headed back to Kimberley that night and alighted from the train the following morning. I was about to walk into an interesting situation...

TROEPIE AND A TIRADE

s I'd mentioned earlier, there were a few new guys making the rounds. None was more musically impressive than Malcolm Du Plessis. An accomplished pianist, he was a burgeoning arranger and producer, and I was going to have some important dealings with him in the next few months. But at first it didn't look like I was going to have any dealings with him at all. To be honest, I knew little about him and had little to no expectation of ever working with him. I knew that some musical was being put together, but not being very Rock 'n Roll in my eyes, I had no interest in it.

That is, until one night, when I was walking past our rehearsal room and a normally quiet and gentle Alan Rolstone came storming out, using a lot of expletives. Puzzled by this behaviour from my friend, I hurried over to where he and a concerned James Thomas, who had followed him outside, were standing.

"I can't work like this! The guy's a complete a**hole! Always wanting to take over, and full of his own opinions! He can't follow instructions from someone who's clearly been put in charge...!!"

Malcolm appeared. "Please come back in Alan!?"

"Malcolm, either you find another guitarist or another cornet player. I can't work with this guy!"

With Malcolm's reassurances ringing in his ears, Alan returned, followed by James and a very curious me. Who could arouse such passion and anger in the mild mannered Rolstone? As I entered, I was struck by the naïveté of such a question. There sat John Ferrier, still arguing the toss about Malcolm's musical arrangement, as if he was the co-producer or co-writer. I got Alan's frustration. Fortunately for me, I found Ferrier's massive ego amusing when I was not in the line of fire. Unfortunately for everyone else in that rehearsal room, these bursts of inspiration and argument that only Ferrier found interesting and profound, were utter time-wasters that interrupted an otherwise great musical score. Malcolm was a teddy bear, but a teddy bear with teeth, and before I knew it, the following morning I was asked to take John's place as the guitarist for the musical TROEPIE. I don't know what John's reaction to his firing was. I can guess, though. He wouldn't believe he was being replaced and would be haranguing Malcolm with questions as to why.

The next night I was handed my score and I settled down to practice. Things went smoothly and everyone, it seemed, was happy. In some ways, this was quite a new experience for me—taking orders from another muso. But I knew that if I played my cards right in this situation and didn't carry on like a Prima Donna, I would be broadening my horizons; after all, I was still leading my guys doing gigs everywhere. Also, I had nothing really to prove and felt quite satisfied with my growing abilities and my share of influence in the musical sphere of the camp. I was being praised particularly for my vocal abilities, which surprised me, because I wasn't that aware of them.

By this time, our company had a new commander who was a particular fan of mine and whose friendship I would take advantage of in a small way when things started to get a bit out of hand in the near future. More of that shortly... In the meantime, we had a musical to perform.

When the evening came, all went swimmingly. Earlier, I had been impressed by Malcolm's ability to actually write music scores for a variety of musical instruments—a feat which made my efforts as a band leader seem positively amateurish. Now I was impressed by his efforts in leading us musically in the capacity of conductor/ music director. What impressed me even more was that none of this seemed to go too much to his head. The popular music world is full of poseurs. To me, the theatrical music world seemed a lot more serious, musically. Ultimately, I still preferred the Pop/Rock music side of things, even if it was a bit pretentious, but right now I was enjoying a new musical experience so I happily rose to the occasion. Themi did a great job showing off his acting talents and the whole evening had an air of professionalism. As I was soon to discover, this was going to be somewhat to my disadvantage... One Friday afternoon in March, after lunch I wandered over to the band bungalow before everyone went back to work, to prep my members for a gig we'd been booked for that evening. I found everyone lounging around in their usual state of narcolepsy, and launched into my dialogue about the night's work that lay ahead. Before I could get much further, Alan looked sleepily at me and informed me that I no longer had a brass section. I thought he was joking. Unfortunately for me, he was not! The reason? My old nemesis, Sergeant Major Second Class, Kaffertjie de Meyer!

Apparently, without any consultation with the rest of the musos in the camp, a brass band had been formed. Did I, as one of two leaders of the now slowly disintegrating Magirus, need to be informed when rehearsals and brass band performances were going to clash with our own band schedule? Apparently not! Was I going to take this lying down? Definitely not! Especially as I now had an ally in Transport 1:1, my old office. That ally was Captain Blignaut, who had no time at all for de Meyer and was more than happy to inform me of his feelings. I stormed out of the bungalow, across the road dividing Transport 1:2 and my basics unit, Maintenance 1:1, straight into Sergeant Major de Meyer! Whether I was mad or stupid, I don't know, but there and then I decided to confront this poison dwarf with the vicious temper. I got the response I was expecting—at first, disbelief that I was actually confronting him about stealing my brass players and not telling me, then a tirade of abuse, threats and bad language.

I stood my ground. "Alright Sergeant Major, let's see what Captain Blignaut has to say about this..." With Kaffertjie hot on my heels, I stormed over to Transport 1:1 and requested an interview with the Captain.

To be honest, I think the Cap was a bit put out by me using our burgeoning friendship and knowledge of his likes and dislikes of his fellow PF's to my advantage in a row such as this. But I needed all the help I could get right now, and as I stood outside in the road with the sergeant major disdainfully commenting on my person to all passersby, I knew full well that this show of bravado was nothing more than a nervous attempt to cover up a grave fear that he was going to be outnumbered in the popularity department in this interview! I smirked the smirk of a man with foreknowledge.

We were ushered into the captain's presence where we both pleaded our cases. I couldn't help but notice how much arse-creeping the sergeant major was doing. He was choosing his words very carefully—as if he was afraid that at any moment the Cap was going to chew him out for just being in his presence. This was a man on the back foot, and I was enjoying every minute of his grovelling. I won't bore you with the details; suffice it to say we came to an arrangement that satisfied both parties, with me getting my brass guys back for the gig, and the sergeant major promising to be a bit more flexible when it came to the needs of Magirus. After all, we were a working band, earning an income for the unit. The only thing the brass band was doing was taking part in competitions—something that James and Alan in particular had little time for.

As we were excusing ourselves from the captain's presence, Kaffertjie turned to me in an effort to re-stamp his authority in what turned out to be a slap-down for him, and said, in as orderly and non-vicious voice as possible, "Clive," (I couldn't believe he'd called me by my first name) "don't ever confront me like this again! Remember your rank, Corporal!"

Did I detect a hint of grudging respect there? I decided to play along and not push my luck too far with this lunatic. "Yes, Sergeant Major." Case closed.

One of the last gigs we did away from Kimberley with our bus was in a place called Kenhardt, a tiny town in the middle of nowhere where all the locals, including a very pretty Afrikaans girl who was watching us, had brown teeth! EVERYONE there had brown teeth—animals and humans alike! It was crazy, and somewhat off-putting. The reason for this, we discovered, was due to the water in the area. The locals called it hard water, and while it was very good for teeth,

BEFORE WE GO FURTHER—
THE RONEO ROOM INCIDENT

━━━◀▶━━━

You might recall I mentioned that I was working in the roneo room with the good natured Rob. The discovery of a piano in the room adjacent had me sneaking in and composing music as often as I could—even in the middle of the day when I was supposed to be working. I wrote two songs on that piano, one that wound up on the B side of my first single, *November*. It was called "The Puzzle", a bittersweet love ballad about the general complexities of the women I had been involved with up 'til then—Caroline in particular. The other was a rousing, beer-swilling song called "The Organ Grinders Song" about a poor old organ grinder with a dancing monkey well known in his town but ultimately neglected ignored and finally abandoned by the townsfolk. I loved that piano! It had a surprisingly good action and a beautiful tone to it, and one bright day in February my love for it put me in an extremely precarious situation with the commandant himself!!

I had finished my two pieces and needed an audience to bounce them off. Enter the only audience I had in the roneo room, my friend Rob. Very eagerly, I led him into the piano room and sat down at the piano, thumping out my tunes as if my life depended on it. There was nothing unsure about my performance—I knew these songs were winners; the world just needed to know about them, starting with my roneo room partner in crime! As I was halfway through "The Organ Grinders Song" my elation and concentrated performance were abruptly interrupted by a private yelling through an open window which happened to be diagonally opposite headquarters:

167

"The Commandant's coming!" Before I could even vacate the piano stool, an extremely angry face appeared at the window.

It was the commandant. "Wat die donner gaan hieraan?? Get to my office now!!"

This was serious shit!! The C.O. himself coming to tree us aan. Needless to say, Rob and I were very quickly met by the Adj., Graham Kershaw, who warned us that the commandant was trying to find out whether or not my rank as lance-corporal was substantive. If it wasn't, I was in for a demotion to private! Almost immediately we were frog-marched through H.Q. straight into the commandant's office and placed in front of his desk. A long, angry monologue followed: we were neglecting our duty, I was not worthy of my rank by such actions, this was the army, not high school etc. etc. One comment that ticked me off a bit was the commandant's comment that he didn't expect this kind of behaviour from Rob, because he was a provincial rugby player—the inference being that, because Rob played rugby, he was of obviously better character, and what was he doing hanging around with the likes of me anyway, someone who he (the C.O.) could understand would behave like this?!

After the kakking out, sentence was passed..."Here it comes..." I thought. "Demoted to private!"

Commandant: "Private Rob, you will get one week's extra duties! Korporaal Hay, for two weeks you will dig bottles!! Every day for an hour after work and on Saturday mornings you will dig bottles!!"

Had the man lost his mind? Dig bottles? (Hey man, I really DIG those bottles man...) What was he talking about? I didn't think he was in a mood to answer questions, so I deferred any I had to our Adj. after the interview. Graham informed me that there was a field at the back of the camp that contained a lot of old bottles the camp was trying to clear out, and that I was to take a wheelbarrow and bag to dig up any old bottles and glass for disposal. Ah! Understanding is the best thing in the world, to quote an old song. Actually, the punishment was meant to demean me to the kind of things that were expected of roofs. This C.O. really didn't like me too much.

But I'm not one to be dismayed by this kind of thing, and my first foray into bottle land was interesting to say the least. Firstly, it gave me time alone, which I quite enjoyed. Secondly, those bottles!! They had a treasure chest back there! I was digging up bottles of the most amazing colour, shape, and size—and many were from the turn of the century!

I had done about two days of my punishment when Saturday morning came around. Admittedly, Saturday morning was a hard one for me to swallow. I almost always went into town with the lads, and today I was going to miss out. Wandering up to the field, I was soon surprised by a visit from Graham Kershaw. We got chatting and I soon discovered that under his Dudley Do Right exterior Graham was a pretty nice guy. As our conversation continued, I noticed our commandant viewing us from the car. Thing is, in his eyes, Graham could do no wrong, so with a scowl and some reluctance at our friendly banter, he drove away. The time was about 11am.

Being the chancer that I was, I asked, "Graham, are you OK if I go to town?"

With a furtive glance over his shoulder and a friendly grin at the cheekiness of the question, he assented: "Yes, OK... Get out of here". That was the last time I dug bottles.

AEROSOL THE BRICKS

ne of the more melancholy things happening during those last six months in Kimberley was the slow unravelling of our band, Magirus. Strangely enough, or maybe in some ways, obviously enough, it was reflected in our sleeping arrangements. From the time the captain had thrown this lot of degenerates together we had always been in one bungalow. Now, with the sun slowly setting on our little orchestra, we had, at the beginning of my final six months, been moved to a room adjacent to our music/ practice room. While this was convenient, I couldn't help but notice how it was slowly being eroded of personnel, until, about six weeks before my departure, I was the only one left in this room.

We had done so much together as a group, not only musically, but socially as well. Part of our journey together had involved musical excursions to see and interact with some giants of South African music at the time; people like the superb guitarist Johnny Fourie, who held a workshop at Kimberley's local music store (the one where Vincent had first laid eyes on his Fender Rhodes). Discovering the band Toto together (courtesy of Malcolm) one weekend while driving back into Johannesburg from Jan Smuts airport (as it was then known) around February of my last six months. All of us meeting up at a movie theatre in Joburg to watch "Sgt. Pepper's Lonely Hearts Club Band" with the Bee Gees, Earth Wind and Fire et al. Our trip to the local township in Kimberley the previous October to see Pacific Express in concert, an extraordinary Coloured light jazz band from Cape Town led by singer Zane Adams. This concert was particularly interesting for two reasons: firstly, we stood out like sore thumbs in the audience in our brown uniforms, blue berets and short hair.

Secondly, because a rather unwelcome spotlight was about to be trained on yours truly!

The audience, as it was , was predominantly Coloured, and we were treated to as much humiliation as they could bravely muster. Shouts of "Die Boere is hier" (The Boers are here), among other slights and insults, suddenly made me realize what it may be like to be on the receiving end of racial slurs—particularly seeing as I was decidedly NOT a Boer! But this is the nature of racism—it lumps a group of people together and decides they're all the same. My feelings of inadequacy were further compounded when, by some strange twist of fate, I had to get up on stage with Pacific Express. I wish I could tell you that the reason for my sudden fame was that they suddenly realized that they had in their midst one of similar fame, talent and ability. Alas, this was not the case. I was whisked up to the stage because, when we had bought our tickets for the concert, they came with a number for a draw the organisers had put on to win a prize. The draw happened right in the middle of the concert, and by some incredible stroke of misfortune, my ticket had the winning number! Somewhat bewildered, and urged on by my fellow band-mates, I made my way to the platform. What no-one had told us was that the prize was an album by Pacific Express, which, in order to claim, I would have to name! Zane, clearly enjoying the fact that he had a "Boer" onstage with him, proceeded to ask me what the name of the album was...A slight aside here. Like most white South Africans, I had intimate knowledge of our heroes' albums. Ask me the names, dates, and songs of any album by my heroes Yes, Genesis, Supertramp, or any you may care to name that I was vaguely familiar with, and I would not only give you that information, but I'd embellish it with who produced it, who did the album artwork, which company released it under which label etc., etc. Ask me the name, however, of anything relating to South African music other than the best known South African songs and artists, and, I'm ashamed to say, I was hopeless! With cries of "Hy's 'n Boer" (He's a Boer) ringing out from the audience, Zane tried in vain to get the required answer out of me, to no avail. He resorted to whispering the name to me, which I finally picked up and answered, before being shunted off back to my seat, prize in hand.

One of the funniest things that happened during my twilight months in the new sleeping quarters was my introduction to Ian Dury and the Blockheads. I say it was funny, but at the time, it was a rather rude awakening from a blissful sleep. I'd drifted off rather early that night with some of the others quietly moving around. The lights were on, which didn't really bother me—one learns to sleep in many different circumstances in the army! The next thing I knew, someone was shouting some expletives in a very loud voice in our room, which woke me with a start! My sleep-funked brain was trying to decipher this outburst. Being shouted at like this in the middle of sleeping was very common in the army, usually by our instructors. But this was around February or March in my last six months— not my basics of eighteen months prior! Also, the voice that was emanating from what I slowly realized was one of our amplifiers, had a very strong Cockney accent, with the expletives followed by some bizarre music. The next thing I knew, Malcolm and a couple of the others came bursting through the door in hysterical laughter. I had just been introduced to the Blockhead's "Plaistow Patricia". I can't remember how many times we all repeated the introduction (some of which is too rude to mention in such a polite book as this), falling about in hysterics all the while. Some of the lyrics of that introduction found their way into our consciousness and stayed there right up to the present, particularly the curtly delivered "oh OH".

I have to doff my hat here to the Seventies. I was extremely blessed to be a teenager in the Seventies—and a teenager with a love and ambition for music in that decade. John Lennon famously said "Weren't the Seventies a drag?!" Whether or not he was referring only to the politics of the Seventies, I have no idea, but if he was referring to the music of the time, I'd say he was severely out of touch! If the Fifties had given us a musical revolution in the form of Rock 'n Roll, and the Sixties had freed us a little further with its forays into Rock, the Seventies opened the fullest music tapestry that modern music has ever seen—then and now. As a collective generation, we all

LOVED and sang along to ABBA, Billy Joel, Bread, Black Sabbath, Cat Stevens, Camel, the Carpenters, the Eagles, Elton John, Jethro Tull, Pink Floyd, the Bee Gees, Earth Wind and Fire, Gino Vanelli, Genesis, Led Zeppelin, Al Jarreau, Randy Crawford, The Sex Pistols, The Clash, Dire Straits, Yes, and so many others. The fact that we all liked such a vastly different array of music was largely due to the fact that music was allowed to breathe and be experimental in that decade. Musicians in these bands taught us that, in order to make it in the world of music, you had to be able to play an instrument more than proficiently. That songwriting was a true art form in which the simple and complex complimented each other, and poetry in lyricism was highly prized and to be emulated. I think it is a decade that has been severely underrated and largely ignored in so many ways. We were allowed, by these bands, to be headbangers, romantics, philosophers and heroes all at the same time. Music of the Seventies made us men and women of great complexity and character, and, as we aged and raised families, allowed us to be treated with respect by our children, who see the value of its impact even upon them and their heroes, in this age of a largely supercilious musical generation.

Even with the slow disintegration of our band I managed to thrive and survive, just as the army expected of us, albeit on their terms. We had made our mark in that unit, and that gave us certain freedoms that I doubt others of our rank and status had experienced before.

THE AUTUMN OF
MY CONTENT

———————◆◆———————

You can only hope when you start out in life that you get a good start in your chosen career. I hadn't quite made up my mind whether I wanted to pursue music professionally or not. I knew I wanted to be involved, but still lacked the confidence to take the leap of faith. I knew where to go if I wanted to take that leap, however. On our classic weekend in Joburg with the band those months ago, Vincent took me to the Don Hughes Organisation on the Friday afternoon before Debbie's Matric Farewell gig. DHO were probably the biggest music agency in Joburg, and probably in the country at the time, and Vincent introduced me to Maurice, Josie, Carol and Corrine, to whom I was going to be professionally tied for the next twenty-one years, though I didn't know it at the time. In many ways I already had a great start with Magirus. I had the comfort of being surrounded by some pretty awesome musos, and the advantage of honing my instrumental, vocal and leadership skills at the same time. There was one area in music that I needed experience in, and that was in the music studio doing some recording. Enter our old commanding officer, Captain Charles Stevens.

Sometime early in April, the Cat, as we called him (aka Cat Stefans, Cat Stevens) called a meeting to tell us he had decided that there was a gap in the music market he was destined to fill! He had shown us newspaper clippings from his pre-army days in opera circles in Cape Town ("Stevens wins acclaim" etc.) and decided that with the country's top two tenors out of the way (Ge Korsten was in career limbo and Gert Potgieter had died), the world was waiting for him to step in. To kick-start his career, he decided that he should do an album, and that no expense, at least to the army, should be spared. Malcolm du Plessis was chosen to play piano, do the song arrangements, and to choose and lead the band. The recording venue—EMI studios in Johannesburg! Wow!! Many of the musicians were a shoe-in. Aubrey Boltman was on keys, Alan, James and some newer guys were on brass, but the search now started for a rhythm section. Once again, I didn't consider myself a shoe-in on guitar. John Ferrier was in many ways a superior player in certain genres than I was, and was to prove himself after our army stint in spades with top SA pop outfit Four Jacks and a Jill, with whom he is still associated today. The general consensus between Malcolm and the Cat was that, temperamentally and chops-wise, I was the better choice for this type of music, and so I got the call.

Although I wasn't that concerned about whether I got the gig or not, I kind of suspected I might, only because I could follow instructions without wanting to take over. Serious compliments were flowing, and I started to realise that a door was opening up before me. I was on the threshold of my life's path, and this opportunity was pushing me to take my first real steps.

Recording was scheduled for the last week in May, so we had plenty of time to rehearse. In the meantime, there was lots of jolling to be done.

My dating regime at that stage was somewhat varied. I was hanging out more and more at the Drake's house, and was somewhat taken with the quiet, patient and understanding Glenda, who was in her final year at school. Glenda was great company for me, and was my "main girl" for the rest of my stay in Kimberley. There was never more than kissing between us, something that, if it bothered her, she never said anything about. I was happy with that state of affairs for a few reasons: firstly, I didn't want to get deeply involved with someone I was barely, if ever, going to be seeing in the future. Secondly, I didn't want to be tied down, because there was the most unusual girl I was having sexual flirtations with at the Kimberley Sun, where she worked as a receptionist. I say flirtations, because she wouldn't let me get past third base, which I found incredibly provocative and frustrating at the same time. One night found us both stark naked in a suite at the Kimberley Sun, never quite totally consummating our passion because she would only let me go so far. I ended it soon enough—what a way to carry on!! There was also Sandy (not my original Sandy—a Jewish girl who was very keen and who I dated casually) and her friend, Vanessa, on whom I was very keen, but who was only fleetingly keen on me. Thirdly, I still had the ghost of Caroline lingering around the corners of my mind, occasionally coming back to haunt me and never quite allowing me to move on completely...my hollow victory lingering in a sea of what ifs... Poor Glenda, what a mixed up, confused Sad Sack to be dating!! Still, I wasn't really complaining... If life had been a cakewalk those past twelve months, the final few months were a cornucopia. As an NCO I had certain privileges, like eating at the NCO's mess, which catered not only for the likes of me, but also for the PF sergeant majors and all the other NCOs in the unit. The food was consequently more than a cut above the private's NSM mess, and the chef, who was a staff sergeant himself, made sure we were well catered for.

It was also about this time that the powers that be decided that all the officers in the unit—COs and NCOs, PFs and NSMs—had to participate in a formal dinner. This was to take place in the camp's hall on a Friday evening, and turned out to be the first of two that we had to attend. The second one was held about a month later, and at the second one we were allowed to bring dates, but we had to get through the first one... I was a little trepidacious at the thought of being surrounded by a bunch of PFs trying to act hoi poloi when they generally acted like animals wherever there was alcohol in the vicinity, and part of any formal dinner always includes alcohol! To be honest, none of us really had a clue what a formal dinner was about, so it was with some surprise, mirth and enjoyment that we attended a compulsory training session about a week before the dinner. Our instructor was one of my favourite sergeant majors, WO2 Vermeulen, who was fair, friendly and had a great sense of humour. I was also surprised at how much knowledge he had about the etiquette of a formal dinner, as in many ways he was a rough diamond. We learned which cutlery to use for each course, which plates were for specific courses, from which direction things were passed at the table, which alcohol gets consumed at which time and with which dish etc. For Hughie, Eddie, who had in the meantime been promoted to lance-corporal as well, and myself, it was a chance to act posh ourselves, whilst pretending to be important—well at least more important than the roofs and the older privates.

The night of the dinner rolled around, and we all converged on the entrance of the hall to be served our first aperitif—sherry. About fifteen minutes later we were ushered into the hall to be seated and served our first course, a fish dish along with a fine Chardonnay. Four courses were served in total, along with whichever wine or alcoholic drink was appropriate to that dish. In between all this, we ordered beer, and consequently got thoroughly drunk! The evening ended with a fortified wine, which just put the final nail in the drinking coffin. Needless to say, I rolled out of that hall back to our bungalow, and managed to stagger convincingly with Hughie, suggesting that we head out to our regular, the Kimberley Sun. Apparently he could hold his liquor better than I could, because when we got back to the bungalow I collapsed on the bed, and for the first time in my drinking life, the room started spinning with me complaining that I wanted to vomit. I've never forgotten that feeling to this day, and while I had been drunk before, this was a new experience. With Hughie rapidly losing patience with me I saw no way of picking myself up in the state I was in to go jolling at the Kimberley Sun. I lay there for a few more moments, when miraculously, my nausea passed and I felt better. Struggling up, I called to Hughie who was on his way out already, to hold on, and off we went to continue the party.

After the joys and indulgences of our first ever formal dining experience, the powers that be decided that a second formal meal was a good idea. This was not so much a dinner as a lunch, and was held in the NSM's mess. My date was a sexy Jewish girl, Michelle, who I'd been seeing quite a bit of in between visits to Glenda. We'd gone out a couple of times to movies and drinks, and I was actually quite taken with her—that is, until the day of the formal dinner/

lunch! To my embarrassment, and in front of a newly engaged Mike Coote and Diane McLaughlin, as well as the rest of the officer/NCO corps, gorgeous Michelle proceeded to embarrass me by giggling inanely through all four courses. For some reason she couldn't help herself, and not wanting to make a scene, I bore the condescending stares. That was pretty much the last time I saw her...

THE RETURN OF THE NATIVE

y time in Kimberley was rapidly drawing to a close, and there was the ever-so-slight romantic temptation to stay on as a civilian and live as a free man in the town that had been so much a part of my life in the last two years. It is something that a few of my friends did after their tenure with the SANDF. As I half-toyed with the idea, I knew that the urge to prove myself in the field of local music was driving me forward, and besides, it was time to move on. Kimberley and the army had had me for two years of my life, and like a servant who had grown to know his master's weaknesses, I had exploited them to the hilt, knowing that my tenure in this household held no surprises or anything that would benefit me going forward.

Time was drawing closer for our recording debut in Joburg, and before we knew it, we were on our way. Approximately five weeks before I klaared out we found ourselves in the big smoke once again. Having rehearsed ourselves sick over the weeks, we were finally ready to lay down our tracks at EMI. What was particularly exciting about working here was that local heroes Clout recorded at this very studio, with the very engineer, Ian Martin, who was going to turn our music and the captain's singing into a masterpiece! All girl group Clout had had a massive hit with "Substitute" in the UK, Europe and Australasia as well as at home, and here we were, a bunch of yokels from the army, recording our debut album with the Cat in the very same studio as these big stars!

This time, my visit home, in spite of the joyful gravity of the occasion, left me hanging somewhat. My mom and stepfather had informed me that they were moving to Hong Kong, which left me feeling somewhat insecure as to what life held in store for me. It was a combination of an exciting and scary time, with the only assurance being that I was moving back to my beloved Joburg to launch myself into my adulthood. On my own. Alone...

Ian van der Linde was with us while we were recording. Not being involved with the project, for some reason he'd just come along for the ride, but I well remember him, Alan and me treating ourselves to a Cabaret show at the top of the Carlton—quite possibly the poshest place in Joburg at the time. The artist's name was Sloopy—I always remembered her name because it seemed to me to be a combination of the words Sloppy and Droopy. She was a cockney girl with a great voice, but with a somewhat Music Hall approach to her act, and the setting was very quiet and intimate—too intimate for three army guys trying to fit into a classy place and being serenaded with semi-classy entertainment. But that was the problem with Joburg—a lot of money and not a lot of class. One night after a recording session, a few of us had been drinking at the clock bar at the Carlton Centre, and I wound up at a phone box, somewhat dronk-verdriet (crying-drunk), with a sudden urge to hear a friendly voice. The first person that came to my dialling finger was Debbie. We were still great friends, so in the state I was in I decided, of course, to declare my undying love to her. We still laughed at our original breakup, but for her it was fairly traumatic at the time, and it took her a while before she could talk to me without yelling obscenities at me. But we were solid when we got it all sorted out, and at that drunken moment, I wondered whether I had made a huge mistake by breaking up with her. Having a great sense of humour, and obviously realising the state I was in, she graciously heard me out, and equally graciously turned me down. She went on to marry a good friend of mine, Brett Schafer, and I was a witness to the start of their very successful and loving married life together. Very sadly, Debbie died of cancer in 2012. She was a wonderful girl and a good friend.

In the midst of all the excitement of being in Joburg again, we managed to sneak away to see other acts, like the night that saw a few of us heading to the Branch Office club to watch what was quite possibly the best band around at the time. Called Backtrax, they consisted of probably the best lineup of session musos in Joburg at the time. Lofty Schultz on sax, the mooning Eric Norgate on trumpet, Glyn Storm on keys, Malcolm Watson on guitar, Les Goode (who was later to grace one of my biggest singles) on bass, Kevin Kruger on drums and John Weddepohl on vocals; these guys were playing all the big, complicated jazz pop songs of our day. We were in awe. In fact, much of our time that trip was spent going around watching the best that Joburg had to offer musically, feasting our ears and eyes on people who actually knew a few modes and scales other than major, minor and pentatonic ones. We were in our musical element and hungry to get as much as we could, while we could.

The recording session itself was a learning curve, but everything went pretty much according to plan. Our final lineup of musicians consisted of four brass players—Alan, James, Mike Bayes and Robert Bailey, the very affable and amusing Dale Collins on drums, Themi on bass guitar, Malcolm and Aubrey taking care of the keyboard parts, and yours truly on guitar. Walking into the hallowed premises of EMI in President Street was both scary and awe-inspiring at the same time, and we managed to get through most of our songs in one take, and I'm happy to say I acquitted myself well in both our band sessions and in my solo sections. I guess it was the comfort of belonging, and the fact that we all were extremely well rehearsed. Going up to the sound desk and listening back to our work, we were akin to a bunch of quiet four-year-olds, eagerly listening to a story being read to us, although this time we were the authors. Malcolm impressed everyone with his command of and interest in all things studio-wise. His only bug bear was the onerous task of trying to get a drunk captain to sing in tune to every one of the songs he performed for the album, which puzzled me at first as I was always taken with his own rhetoric about what a star he was! Ah, arrogance and privilege— two things that don't line up when the rubber meets the road. The only sour note for me was an invitation from Ian Martin for us to drop in on a Clout recording session, but when we later took him up on it, he was visibly irritated with our presence there, an experience that left me feeling unwelcome and uneasy in the presence of any big studio or recording personnel for some time. It was something I got over soon enough, however. I had studio plans of my own—but that's another story.

I took the opportunity of being in Joburg to say goodbye to my parents who were leaving for their own adventure, and sad farewells were said at Jan Smuts international airport. Actually, it was sadder for my mom than for me. My mom was leaving behind everyone and everything she knew and loved for a life in a foreign country—something I would experience myself some twenty years later, only to realise how hard that can be. She had a good life in Hong Kong and was away for fifteen years, returning to South Africa for six short years before moving to the UK where she currently resides.

We finished the recording at EMI and headed back to Kimberley, being mindful of the fact that there were only a few short weeks left before I klaared out. For some reason, I missed the photo shoot for the back of the album cover, and wound up having to be inserted into the photo. Actually, I was happy with this at the time because the photo I submitted for the insert had me sitting with a pair of earphones on and playing my beloved Ibanez twelve-string, a photo taken by someone when we were actually doing the recording. Contrasting this was the main photo, which consisted of all the band members in full stepout (formal) uniform standing behind a seated, unsmiling and rather curt looking Charles Stevens. Even though I was wearing the band's notorious tracksuit top with the two yellow stripes running down both arms, I looked positively cool by comparison.

But here I was, elated, excited and slightly apprehensive, on the threshold of my civilian life...

AND NOW THE END IS NEAR

The old Frank Sinatra song "My Way" was a number we did with regularity at our gigs with Magirus, and if I was to make a change to it, it would be to the title... "My Way" would become "Our Way", because that is what we got a lot of the time in Kimberley—from the personnel at the camp to our lovers, friends and fans. Not that it was all taking and no giving—we gave our music, our time, our love and friendship, as well as our lives in service for that two year period, and it has reaped a lifetime of achievement, comradeship and beautiful memories. But the time was coming to an end, and my last few weeks at camp were somewhat disconnected. We were in something of a no-man's-land, our status downgraded to the point where I had to berate a new instructor corporal to watch his attitude towards us, much to the amusement and admiration of John Ferrier. And yet everyone knew we were the "ou manne", or old guard, just biding our time before we klaared out. What was really odd and perhaps a little sad for me was watching some of the guys who I did basics with as they returned in preparation for their klaaring out. A lot of them had been on the border, and for them, coming back to camp was an experience in itself. I saw a lot of bewildered stares as these guys returned to relative civilization—something we had been used to for two years, but for them, was an amazing sight.

I felt somewhat sorry for Alan, James and the others, who still had six months to go, but for the likes of Kevin, Ferrier, Pete Auths and myself, we were getting ready for the world... There was one more little chapter to the Magirus story, and fittingly, it involved my old nemesis Kaffertjie de Meyer. A lot of the NSM loots were also klaaring out and, seeing as many of them liked us and had travelled this journey alongside us, they requested a final gig at the Jack Hindon NSM officers quarters, part of the Danie Theron Combat School complex, on our very last night in camp. Interestingly, it was Graham Kershaw who asked me to organise it. As I mentioned, we had become pretty good friends, with him finally accepting my AWOL activities. We went through to Jack Hindon that afternoon to set up, and if I thought WE had it good, I had been living in a dream world! Admittedly, we weren't officers, so our quarters were nowhere near as nice as this four star hotel that the officers lived in. They did, however, have a lot more responsibility than we did, and because of their rank, were that much more beholden to the cause of the SANDF—a responsibility I was only too keen to pass up. There was plenty of comfort waiting at home...oh, wait, there was no home to go to...but I wasn't thinking too far ahead, and besides, my very well-off uncle and aunt had agreed to put me up while I found my feet... I digress. The main thing was that these guys were big fans and lent us every assistance in setting up and making sure we were comfortable that night.

After dinner, the very last one I was going to eat in this place, Pete Auths, Dave Oldham, Hughie, Eddie and I headed out for our final Magirus gig. Was I sad? Not a jot! The reality of our last gig together was more a catalyst for my departure than for any feelings of nostalgia. Indeed, I felt like I was in the leather of a catapult that had been pulled back to capacity, just waiting to be propelled into the hereafter, which in this case was the end of my carefree existence, and the beginning of my life as a professional, working musician. And man, did we rock! I remember being so confident of what we were doing because we were such a tight outfit. For some reason, I remember doing "Hotel California" in particular—strangely ironic, seeing as it was one of the songs I was singing on my journey into Diskobolos all those months ago.

Then disaster!! My amp blew. There was nothing I could do about it, and we had a restless crowd waiting. The trouble was, earlier that day when we wanted to get hold of some of our old band equipment, we were informed that it was off limits to us because Kaffertjie had locked it up and was now in charge of whoever was using it. Graham approached me and asked me what the problem was. I told him my amp had blown and that the only place I could get another was at the back of the stage in the camps hall, locked in a storeroom.

He just said "Come with me!!"

We hopped into his car and sped up to the camp, six kilometres away. Being a good adjutant, he decided to follow protocol and ask Warrant Officer 2nd class de Meyer for permission to grab another amp, as well as the key to get it from the storeroom. We arrived and hopped out at Kaffirtjie's house and knocked on the door; the time was 9:30pm—not too early, but certainly not too late in the night either. After about five minutes of knocking with no-one answering the door, we drove across the road and decided to investigate the state of security at the hall. There was no way we were getting in! As we were about to leave I noticed that the window to the storeroom was open...

I said to Graham: "That's where all the gear is..." We both looked up—the storeroom was about one storey up from ground level—and, grabbing a table from the guardhouse, I was just able to reach the latch and haul myself in. I looked at Graham. "Ja, let's do this Clive! I'm not going to let this ruin our night."

"What about Kaffertjie?" I asked somewhat apprehensively.

"Don't you worry about him. I'll tell him myself."

Graham called over the young roof NSM standing guard: "You know who I am?"

"Ja Lieutenant."

"You're sure?"

"Ja Lieutenant."

"OK, we have to go through the window into the storeroom to get an amplifier because the sergeant major has the key to the hall and we can't wake him up. We will return the amplifier tomorrow. Is that clear?"

"Ja Lieutenant."

"Good. Get back to your duty when we have finished."

In I went, and looking around brought back a flood of memories—the old organ with the beautiful Leslie speaker, our old amps, the Fender Rhodes that the Cap had bought for Vincent, it was all here—most of the gear we were using at tonight's gig was our own. I was standing in a veritable Magirus museum, gazing at this gear for the last time. I took just enough time to reflect before Graham called out to see if everything was OK. I grabbed a guitar amp, climbed through the window, and we headed back to Danie Theron to finish the gig... It had been two years of pain, pleasure, triumph and disappointment, with a bunch of emotions totally new to all of us thrown in for good measure. I'd arrived with little but my talent and emerged with more experience in what became my chosen field than did most NSMs who were sequestered in that two year vacuum. I'd learned what it was to lead and follow, what it was to meet my match in the game of love, what it meant to win and lose, and that my talent was a precious thing to nurture and grow. I'd learnt that we will always have friends and enemies, but if you stick together, nothing can move you. I'd learned that everyone has different strengths and weaknesses, and that we were all a small sum of the whole part. Most importantly, I'd learned that whatever life throws at you, throw yourself back and charm the socks off people while you do it! In fact, I'd become a good soldier...certainly not in the way the SANDF envisaged, but rather in the lessons of life. And so on the eve of my departure, I could honestly say that the army had done its job...

The final day dawned, and fittingly, and somewhat surprisingly, we were treated to a farewell lunch at the NSM's mess where a fairly formal speech was given by the RSM. We ate, then headed back to our bungalows to get our personal instruments, suitcases and trommels. As I was leaving the mess, a rather irritated SM de Meyer came towards me: "Korporaal Hay, where are the keys to the Hall?"

"Didn't Lieutenant Kershaw get them from you? I think he has them, Sergeant Major..."

"Well, was the amplifier returned to the hall?"

"I don't know Sergeant Major, we left it down at Danie Theron with the lieutenant for safekeeping..."

"So you didn't return it to the camp?"

"No, we had nowhere to store it here."

A pause. A look of helpless frustration. "Get out of my sight, Mr. Hay!!" he exploded.

"With pleasure, Sergeant Major" I said with a grin.

He stormed off and out of my life...

I've never had such a joyous goodbye in my life. John, Pete, Kevin and I said our farewells and promised to stay in touch. Hugh, Dave, Ian, James, Nick, Eddie and I shook hands warmly and exchanged phone numbers. Alan was in Potch on pass and I was going to pick him up on the way home so we could have a jol in Joeys before he went back to camp.

I loaded my Volkswagen Panelvan and headed Northeast towards Johannesburg with the sun setting behind me.

THE END

www.ingramcontent.com/pod-product-compliance
Lightning Source LLC
Chambersburg PA
CBHW071431090426
42737CB00011B/1631